Airport Spotting Hotels

DestinWorld publishing

Matt Falcus

First Edition 2016

The information in this book is true and complete to the best of our knowledge. All recommendations are made without any guarantee on the part of the Publisher, who also disclaims any liability incurred in connection with the use of specific details or content within this book.

British Library Cataloguing-in-Publication Data
A catalogue record for this book is available from the British Library.

ISBN 978-0-9930950-6-1

Published by Destinworld Publishing Ltd.
www.destinworld.com

Contents

4

Airport Spotting Hotels

Introduction

For those lucky enough to travel in order to pursue their hobby of spotting or photographing aircraft, the research done before a trip nearly always now involves finding a suitable 'spotting hotel'. This is quite a new phenomenon among the spotting community, but can make a trip so much more worthwhile. It is my hope that this book will help facilitate that and make the most of your travels, no matter where they take you.

Airport Spotting Hotels is intended as a reference guide to every airport in the world that features at least one hotel with views of aircraft coming and going or, in the best cases, on the ground. Whilst it is rarer to find one which is suitable for good aircraft photography, they do exist. Nevertheless, most facilitate spotting, and when combined with technology such as SBS units or flight tracking websites, can add a lot of numbers to the book, particularly when you have retired to your room for the night, or when the weather makes it difficult to go outside.

Naturally the details can change, with hotels closing down or changing ownership, or new buildings appearing which obscure views. I will be updating this book whenever possible to keep up with these changes, and any relevant information is usually posted on www.airportspotting.com

As always, when staying at hotels remember that they can not always accommodate your requests for rooms with views, and in many countries this hobby is not understood – especially when electronic equipment, binoculars and telephoto lenses are pointed at windows. As with the well-publicised case in Delhi's Radisson Blu hotel where a maid reported spotters to the authorities, discretion is key even when in the safety of your hotel room.

Matt Falcus

Abu Dhabi

Abu Dhabi International

Premier Inn Abu Dhabi Airport

Opposite Terminal 3, Abu Dhabi Airport 95219
+971 2 818 6666
www.premierinn.com

The rooftop pool area of this hotel, which is linked to the passenger terminal, has excellent views over the aircraft movements. Until recently it was perfectly acceptable to take great photographs and log movements, but the local police have now banned it. So if you use this hotel, discretion is mandatory and the hotel staff may ask you to stop spotting. Aircraft parked at the FBO are not visible, and military aircraft are hard to read because of heat haze. Once the midfield terminal opens, the views may not be as good.

Argentina

Buenos Aires Aeroparque

Hotel Aeroparque Inn and Suites

Av Rafael Obligado Costanera, 1425 CABA, Argentina
+54 11 4803 6002
www.hotelaeroparque.com

Aircraft approaching Aeroparque's runway from the south pass right by this hotel and rooms on the third floor facing north have great views of the action. You can also walk from the hotel to the perimeter of the airport, where spotters often congregate to watch aircraft.

Australia

Cairns

Mercure Cairns Harbourside

209-217 The Esplanade, Cairns North QLD 4870
+61 7 4080 3000
www.mercure.com

A mile or so south of the airport. Aircraft approaching from the south pass low over the hotel and can be read off. Aircraft departing over the hotel can be tracked using SBS or flight tracker websites.

Melbourne

Park Royal Airport Hotel

Arrival Drive, Melbourne Airport, Melbourne, VIC 3045
+61 3 8347 2000
www.parkroyalhotels.com

You can walk directly into this hotel from the terminals via a covered walkway. Rooms can be a bit pricey, but some have excellent views over the airport. Ask for those in the ranges 800-825 and 900-925. You can also get views from the ends of the corridors.

Sydney

Rydges Sydney Airport Hotel

8 Arrival Ct, Sydney Airport, NSW 2020
+61 2 9313 2500
www.rydges.com

A good replacement for the closed International Terminal observation deck. Located just behind the terminal, the Rydges has seized the opportunity presented by spotters by providing day access to its panoramic terrace for a fee. You can see and photograph movements around the terminals and runway 16R/34L. Higher rooms facing the same direction have a similar view, and the hotel offers spotters packages which include the best views, food and drink allowance, information sheet, free Wi-Fi and a pair of binoculars!

Stamford Plaza Hotel

O'Riordan St & Robey Street, Mascot NSW 2020
+61 2 9317 2200
www.stamford.com.au

Higher rooms at this hotel offer views along one of the Domestic Terminal piers. You can also see aircraft on two of the runways at an acceptable distance, and aircraft taxiing to the International Terminal. Ask for a room on floors 7 and above.

Austria

Vienna

NH Vienna Airport Hotel

Einfahrtsstrasse 3, Wien Flughafen 1300
+43 1 7015 10
www.nh-hotels.com

The best hotel at Vienna Airport for views of movements. Odd-numbered rooms on the third floor will give views over the apron. Some other higher rooms have views over the 11/29 runway. The hotel is one of the more affordable at the airport, and it is a short walk from the terminal.

Azerbaijan

Baku

Sheraton Baku Airport

Baku Airport
+994 12 437 49 49
www.sheraton.com

This hotel is located close to the terminals. It has a circular shape, with many rooms on the top floor having good views across at least part of the aprons, gates or runways. You should be able to see a lot of the movements by securing an odd-numbered room facing outwards.

Bahrain

Bahrain International

Movenpick Bahrain Airport

143 Road 2403, Bahrain 999
+973 1746 0000
www.movenpick.com

Situated by the lagoon behind the airport terminals and car park. Rooms facing the airport have a distant view of aircraft taking off and using the runway. Photography is not really possible due to the distance.

Belgium

Brussels National

Novotel Brussels Airport

Da vinci laan 25 Bedrijvenzone Diegem-, Vuurberg, 1831
+32 2 620 04 33
www.novotel.com

A short distance from the terminal (use the free courtesy bus), past the DHL and VIP terminals, is the Novotel. It is situated alongside runway 07L threshold and the road which runs around the northern perimeter. Views are quite limited. If you ask for a room facing the airport runway you should see movements on 07L/25R and aircraft parked on the cargo apron on the northern side. Some distant views of aircraft on approach are possible.

Sheraton Brussels Airport

Brussels National Airport, Brussels 1930
+32 27 10 80 00
www.sheraton.com

This is the best hotel option for spotting aircraft at Brussels Airport. Although expensive, rooms have views over the aprons. It is a short walk from the terminal and multi-storey car park location. Photography is not possible from the rooms because of the shutters, however.

Liege

Park Inn by Radisson Liege Airport

Rue de l'Aéroport 14, 4460 Grâce-Hollogne
+32 4 241 00 00
www.parkinn.com

With Liege coming alive at night, it is ideal to have this hotel from where you can keep an eye on the action. Situated next to the passenger terminal, it has rooms overlooking the runway, taxiways and parking ramp. Distant views of the cargo lineup can be had. Ask for a top floor room.

Brazil

Rio de Janeiro Galeão

Linx Hotel

Avenida Vinte de Janeiro, s/n, Rio de Janeiro 21941-900
+55 21 2468 3400
www.gjphotels.com

A fairly new hotel located on the access road to the airport. Although few rooms face the airport, aircraft can be seen at a distance on approach or departure on both runways.

Rio de Janeiro Santos Dumont

Ibis Hotel Santos Dumont

Av. Marechal Camara, 280 - Centro,
Rio de Janeiro - RJ, 20020-080
+55 21 3506 4500
www.ibis.com

Views are restricted. However, odd-numbered top floor rooms facing the airport have limited views of the parking ramps and aircraft taking off.

Novotel Santos Dumont

Av. Mal. Câmara, 300 - Centro, Rio de Janeiro - RJ, 20020-080
+55 21 3506 8500
www.novotel.com

As with its neighbour, the Ibis (see above), this hotel has some limited views of aircraft movements from top floor rooms facing the airport.

Sao Paulo Congonhas

Ibis Hotel Congonhas

R. Baronesa de Bela Vista, 801 – Vila Congonhas,
Sao Paulo 04612-002
+55 11 5097 3737
www.ibis.com

A good value spotting hotel at Congonhas Airport. It is situated next to the terminal, and rooms on higher floors have a great view of all movements. A lounge on the top floor can see arrivals into Guarulhos on a good day.

Sao Paulo Guarulhos

Hotel Matiz Guarulhos

R. Pedro de Tolêdo, 1000 – Jardim Santa Lidia, Guarulhos
+55 11 3411 7000
www.matizhotelguarulhos.com

The Hotel Matiz is great for spotting, as it has a terrace which is perfect for landing shots. However, sometimes this is closed, or requires to you pay for day access if you're not a guest. This hotel is the best option as it has great views of arrivals. Aircraft can be read off from rooms facing the airport.

Canada

Calgary

Delta Calgary Airport Hotel

2001 Airport Rd NE, Calgary Airport, AB T2E 6Z8
+1 403 291 2600
www.deltahotels.com

A new hotel opened in 2014 and linked to the airport terminal. Higher rooms facing the airport have views of aircraft on the runways and around the terminal area.

Edmonton

Renaissance Edmonton Airport

4236 36th Street East, Edmonton, AB T9E 0V4
+1 780 488 7159
www.renaissance.com

A tall hotel linked to the terminal at Edmonton International Airport. Rooms on higher floors looking out over the apron will see some aircraft parked at the northernmost gates, and aircraft using the runways in the distance.

Halifax International

ALT Hotel Halifax Airport

40 Silver Dart Dr, Enfield, NS B2T 1K2
+1 902 334 0136
www.althotels.com

A modern airport hotel situated behind (and linked to) the passenger terminal. It is tall and upper rooms are high enough to see over the terminal to the runways beyond. Not great for photography.

Montreal Pierre Elliott Trudeau

Aloft Montreal Airport

500 Ave., Boulevard McMillan, Monteal, QC H9P 0A2
+1 514 633 0900
www.aloftmontrealairport.com

Ask for a room facing the airport on the fifth floor and you will see the southern runway only a short distance away. The northern runway is also visible in the distance, but often the heat haze will refrain you from reading registrations off.

Best Western Plus Montreal Airport

13000 Autoroute Côte-de-Liesse, Dorval, QC H9P 1B8
+1 514 631 4811
www.bestwestern.com

Set a little further back from the Sheraton (see below), it offers similar views of aircraft on approach to runway 06R. A little too distant for photograph.

Marriott Fairfield

700 Michel Jasmin Ave, Montreal H9P 1C5
+1 514 631 2424
www.marriott.com

This hotel is situated within the terminal buildings. High rooms facing the airport are good for arrivals on runway 06R, and aircraft using the other runway are also visible.

Sheraton Montreal Airport

555 Boulevard McMillan, Montréal, QC H9P 1B7
+1 514 631 2411
www.sheraton.com

This is not a tall hotel, but many of the rooms face towards the adjacent threshold of runway 06R, which makes it good for monitoring aircraft movements.

Ottawa International

Hilton Garden Inn Ottawa Airport

2400 Alert Rd, Ottawa, ON K1V 1S1
+1 613 288 9001
www.hilton.com

The only hotel with views at Ottawa. High level rooms facing the airport look over the First Air and FedEx aprons, and runway 25's threshold beyond. The main runway is in the distance, but movements can be seen and tied up with a flight tracker.

Toronto Pearson International

Hilton Toronto Airport

5875 Airport Rd, Mississauga, ON L4V 1N1
+1 905 677 9900
www.hilton.com

Rooms on higher floors facing the airport give views of aircraft traffic using the runways. Some buildings obstruct views of the furthest runway, but aircraft can usually be seen once airborne from windows in the corridors; rooms ending in 35 or 37 are next to these corridor windows. The hotel is used to requests for views from spotters.

Sheraton Gateway

Terminal 3, Toronto Airport, On L5P 1C4
+1 905 672 7000
www.starwoodhotels.com

A good hotel connected to the terminals with views across the ramp and some of the runways. Terminal 1 is not visible, however most aircraft will taxi into view. Ask for a high level room facing the airport.

ALT Airport Hotel

6080 Viscount Road, Mississauga, ON L4V 0A1
+1 905 362 4337
www.althotels.com

Another option close to the terminals, a high level room facing the airport should give a grandstand view of aircraft movements. It is a little more distant than other hotels, but still possible to read off aircraft.

Vancouver International

Fairmont Vancouver Airport

3111 Grant McConachie Way, Richmond, BC V7B 0A6
+1 604 207 5200
www.fairmont.com

Located in the northern side of the terminal. Ask for a higher room facing the airport and you'll have views of some of the parking gates and movements. Some rooms even have telescopes! Hotel can be expensive.

Vancouver Seaplane Base

Fairmont Waterfront

900 Canada Pl, Vancouver, BC V6C 3L5
+1 604 691 1991
www.fairmonts.com

Rooms in this downtown hotel offer great views over the comings and goings at Vancouver's busy Seaplane Base. Aircraft park at the pontoons next to Harbour Green Park and fly from Vancouver Harbour beyond.

Winnipeg International

Four Points by Sheraton Winnipeg Airport

1999 Wellington Ave, Winnipeg, MB R3H 1H5
+1 204 775 5222
www.fourpointswinnipegairport.com

A convenient hotel for the airport terminal. Ask for a room facing the airport and you will see aircraft on the runways and parked on the southern passenger terminal apron. Terminal developments may obstruct the views.

The Grand Winnipeg Airport by Lakeview

1979 Wellington Ave, Winnipeg, MB R3H 1H5
+1 204 505 0145
www.lakeviewhotels.com

Even more convenient for the terminal. The Grand is a similar size to the Four Points, and has views a little closer to the commuter aircraft side of the terminal. It has similar views of the runways beyond.

Chile

Santiago de Chile

Diego De Almagro Airport Hotel

Avenida Americo Vespucio Oriente 1299, Santiago
+56 2 2230 5600
www.dahoteles.com

Situated next to a large motorway intersection at the southern entrance to the airport. High level, even-numbered rooms offer views of aircraft using both of the runways, with views of 35R particularly good.

China

Beijing Capital

CITIC Hotel Beijing Airport

No 9 Xiao Tianzhu Road, Capital International Airport, Beijing 100621
+86 10 6456 5588
www.citichotelbeijing.com

Has rooms which look over the approach or departure paths of all three runways, depending on which direction is used. SBS or tracking websites will be needed to tie up most movements. Distant views of the terminals are also possible.

Langham Place Hotel

1 Er Jing Road, Terminal 3, Capital International Airport, Beijing 100621
+86 10 6457 5555
beijingairport.langhamplacehotels.com

The best spotting hotel at Beijing Capital is the Langham Place. It is situated close to Terminal 3 and has rooms facing the runways, city skyline, or the lake. Rooms facing the runway look over the approach to runway 01, whilst those facing the lake will have views of aircraft approaching runway 36R, with 36L in the distance. The hotel is a 10-15 minute walk from spotting location 1.

Chengdu

Chengdu Airport Hotel

Shuangliu Int'l Airport, Shuangliu County, Chengdu

Even-numbered rooms on the top three floors (the 10th floor is for family rooms) have good views facing the runway. You can't see any aircraft parking stands, but should see most movements.

Guangzhou Baiyun

Pullman Hotel

Guangzhou Baiyun Airport, 510470
+86 20 3606 8866
www.pullmanhotels.com

Club rooms on the higher floors of this hotel have good views of the runways, which is especially useful if aircraft are landing towards you. If the opposite direction is in use you will see aircraft departing past you. Some parking aprons and the distant FedEx ramp are also visible.

Shanghai Hongqiao

Hong Gang Shanghai Hotel

2550 Hongqiao Road, Shanghai 200335
+86 21 6268 1008

Ask for a high room with number ending in 10 - 910 for example is a good room. Others include 606 and 702. These all face the terminal's parking ramps and are perfect for spotting and photography. The hotel is very reasonably priced.

Boyue Shanghai Hongqiao Airport (Air China) Hotel

No.181, Shen Da San Road, Hongqiao Airport, Shanghain 200335
+86 21 2236 6666
www.zhboyuehotel.com

Situated in Terminal 2, if you get an Executive room on floors 9 and above you have excellent views of movements. You'll see aircraft parked at both of the terminals, plus runway movements and the executive ramp.

Shanghai Pudong

Dazhong Merrylin 'Ease' Hotel Pudong Airport

6001 Yingbin Avenue, Pudong New Area, Shanghai 201202
+86 21 3879 9999
www.dazhongairporthotel.com

This hotel is reasonably priced and has a direct link to the terminal and train station. Rooms on higher floors facing south have views over the taxiways and runways. An SBS is useful for night movements. Rooms 8801, 8802 and 8806 are reportedly good

Ramada Pudong Airport Shanghai

1100 Qi Hang Road, Shanghai 201207
+86 21 3849 4949
www.ramada.com

This hotel is also reasonably priced, but offers much fewer opportunities. Again, ask for a south facing room looking towards the airport, and on a high floor. You will then get distant views of runway movements and terminal views.

Shenzhen Bao'an

Sunway Hotel

Shenzhen Bao'an Airport
+86 755 2730 0888
www.sunwayhotelsz.com

Located outside the original terminals A and B. Even numbered rooms on floors 3 and above face the airport which are quite distant, but take in most movements. This is probably the easiest place to spot at Shenzhen if you aren't in the departures lounge, and hotel staff are aware of the needs of spotters.

Xi'an

Aviation Hotel

Xi'an International Airport, Weicheng District, Xianyang
+86 298 8797100

Situated opposite the passenger terminal. Rooms on floors 8 and 9 are reportedly the best, and you can easily spot aircraft movements even after dark.

Xiamen

Fliport Garden Hotel

115, Xiangyun 3 Road, Gaoqi Int'l Airport Xiamen
+86 592 5708136
www.fliport.com

A tall hotel a few minutes' walk from the airport terminal. Ask for a room facing the airport on the top three floors and you should be able to see enough over the surrounding buildings, including the southern runway threshold and nearer parking stands.

Cyprus

Larnaca

Flamingo Beach Hotel

152 Piale Pasha Avenue, Larnaca
+357 24 828208
flamingohotelcyprus.com

A popular resort hotel on Mackenzie Beach, to the north east of Larnaca Airport. This beach is great for spotting and photographing arrivals, and rooms in the hotel looking towards the approach are perfect (301 and 401 reportedly the best). The hotel also has a rooftop area which is good for watching aircraft.

Czech Republic

Prague

Courtyard by Marriott

Aviatická 1092/8, 161 00 Praha
+420 236 077 077
www.marriott.com

Located in the car park behind the terminal complex. Top floors rooms are high enough to see aircraft movements on the runways and taxiways, although the terminal buildings can get in the way and the position is a little distant for photographs.

Ramada Prague Airport

K Letisti 25a 1067, 160 00 Prague
+420 220 111 251
www.ramada.com

Located amongst the old terminal buildings (present day Terminal 3) at the south eastern corner of the airport. Although it is quite a long way from the main passenger terminals, rooms do have some views of runway 12/30 and the nearby executive parking apron.

Denmark

Billund

Zleep Hotel Billund

Passagerterminalen 4, 7190 Billund
+45 70 23 56 35
www.zleephotels.com

A small budget hotel with four floors to the west of the terminal. Rooms on the top two floors have partial views across the parking apron and runway.

Copenhagen Kastrup

Hilton Airport Hotel

Ellehammersvej 20, Copenhagen 2770
+45 32 501 501
www.hilton.com

The Hilton is linked to the terminal via a covered walkway. Most rooms ending in 31-35 from the 10th floor up offer views, with photography possible.

Egypt

Cairo International

Le Méridien Hotel

Cairo International Airport, Terminal 3, Cairo
+20 2 22659600
www.lemeridiencairoairport.com

This modern hotel is linked to the newer Terminal 3 at Cairo. It is set back a little way, so any views are only possible from the top floor rooms, and these are too far away to be easily read off. You will need flight tracking software. Rooms face either Terminal 3 and the southern runway, or Terminal 1 and the northern runway.

Sharm el-Sheikh

Sonesta Beach Resort

Naama Bay, 2nd Line, Sharm el-Sheikh
+20 69 3600725
www.sonesta.com

Aircraft pass low over the hotel and pool area shortly before landing when using runways 04L/R. Many of the rooms have balconies with views of approaching aircraft.

Hilton Sharks Bay

El-Shaikh Zayed, Sharks Bay, Sharm El-Sheikh
+20 69 3603333
www.hilton.com

Not really close enough for good photos, but many rooms overlook the runways. You should see every movement if you get a room in the new section facing the airport.

Ethiopia

Addis Ababa

Bole Ambassador Hotel

Bole, Addis Ababa 1130
+251 116 18 8284
www.boleambassador.com

A nice hotel alongside the airport, with views of movements and some of the derelict aircraft on the airfield. Room 439C reportedly good, as is the open rooftop which also has views.

Finland

Helsinki Vantaa

Hilton Helsinki Airport

Lentäjänkuja 1, 01530 Vantaa
+358 9 73220
www.hilton.com

The hotel is located directly behind the airport's main terminal complex and is a couple of floors higher than the terminal buildings. There are only outward facing rooms on two sides of the hotel, facing northeast and southwest (the rest face an inner courtyard). For spotting purposes, you will need rooms facing southwest; rooms facing northeast have views blocked by an adjacent building. The top two floors are best, with rooms on the southwest side overlooking final approach to runways 04L/R and many of the terminal stands.

France

Cannes

Hotel Mercure Cannes Mandelieu

6 allée des Cormorans, Cannes LA Bocca, 06150
+33 4 93 90 43 00
www.mercure.com

A fairly small hotel alongside the perimeter fence close to both runways and a taxiway. Some rooms have views of aircraft movements, and you can also get some views from the hotel car park.

Lyon St Exupery

NH Hotel Lyon Airport

BP 202, Aéroport Lyon Saint Exupery, 69125 Lyon
+33 4 72 23 05 50
www.nh-hotels.com

Situated right behind Terminal 1 and next to the TGV station. Views of aircraft on the ground are mostly obscured by the terminal buildings, but aircraft using the runways can be seen at a distance.

Kyriad Hotel

65 Rue du Royaume-Uni, 69124
+33 4 72 23 90 90
www.kyriad.com

A small budget hotel to the south of the terminals. Rooms facing east in the north-south wing have distant views of the cargo apron and aircraft on the runway.

Marseille Provence

Best Western Marseille Airport

Aéroport, 13127 Vitrolles
+33 4 42 15 54 00
www.bestwestern.com

The only hotel with any views of aircraft movements, and it's not great. The Best Western is set far back from the terminals, near the motorway. Its shape means you'll be lucky to find a room with ideal views, and anything you see will be in the distance.

Nantes

Hotel Oceania Nantes

Nantes Atlantique Airport, 44340 Bouguenais
+33 2 40 32 14 14
www.oceaniahotels.com

Set back behind the passenger car parks. Top floor rooms facing the airport have distant views, sometimes obscured by trees, of some of the commuter aircraft stands and runway 12 threshold beyond.

Nice Cote d'Azur

Campanile Hotel

459-461 promenade des Anglais L'Arénas, 06200 Nice
+33 493 21 20 20
www.campanile.com

Situated opposite Terminal 1 at the airport. Ask for a room on floor 5 facing the airport and you'll have views of aircraft movements and the runways. Not great for photography.

Suite Novotel Nice Airport

125 Boulevard René Cassin, 06200 Nice
+33 4 92 29 41 00
www.accorhotels.com

Set back behind Parc Phoenix. Rooms facing the airport have distant views of aircraft on the runways, with room numbers 614, 615, 714 and 715 reportedly the best.

Hotel Premiere Classe

385 Prom. des Anglais, 06200 Nice
+33 892 70 72 29
www.premiereclasse.com

High floor rooms facing the airport look down over the biz jet parking apron and the runways 22L/R thresholds, so you can see most movements easily. Palm trees on the road and wire mesh fence get in the way of photographs.

Paris Charles de Gaulle

Hilton Paris Charles de Gaulle

Roissypôle, Rue de Rome, Tremblay-en-France 95708
+33 1 49 19 77 77
www.hilton.com

Situated between the two terminal areas. Rooms on the fourth floor or higher offer views of the taxiways and some aprons – particularly rooms ending in 01 and 29. Windows next to the elevators also give views over the holding points.

Roissy Aéroport Cedex

Ibis Hotel

Roissypôle, Roissy 95701
+33 1 49 19 19 19
www.ibishotel.com

A more affordable option is the large Ibis hotel. North facing rooms have views over Terminal 2 and northern runways, and south facing have views over Terminal 1 and the charter terminal. The hotel is also located next to the Mound spotting location.

citizenM

7 Rue de Rome, Tremblay-en-France 93290
+33 1 78 90 26 53
www.citizenm.com

A recent addition, with 'Runway View' rooms that offer a view of the northern runways and the taxiways linking Terminal 2. However, a new building has appeared alongside recently which has limited the number of rooms with a view. It's a short walk from the Mound, and has free Wi-Fi in all rooms.

Paris Le Bourget

Hôtel Kyriad Prestige Le Bourget – Aéroport

Aeroport Du Bourget Zone D'Aviation Affaires, 93350 Le Bourget
+33 1 49 34 10 38
www.kyriad.com

Not to be confused with the smaller Kyriad in Le Bourget Centre, which has no rooms with views, this large airport hotel is to the north of the museum and hangars. Its views are somewhat obscured by surrounding buildings, but high level rooms do have sight of aircraft movements coming and going and at some points on the ground.

Paris Orly

Hilton Paris Orly

Rue Clément Ader, 94390 Paray-Vieille-Poste
+33 1 45 12 45 12
www.hilton.com

Set back from the Ouest Terminal at Orly. Rooms facing west have better views, looking towards the terminal and runway 06/24. You won't see everything, and photography is no good. But the hotel is a short walk from the viewing areas in the terminals.

Toulouse Blagnac

Campanile Hotel Toulouse Blagnac

3 Avenue Didier Daurat, 31700 Blagnac
+33 5 61 16 90 90
www.campanile.com

A couple of miles south of the terminals in the Purpan district. Although it has no views of the airport itself, when aircraft are arriving from the south they pass fairly low overhead. Only rooms facing south can see aircraft, however. Easily accessible on the motorway.

Germany

Berlin Tegel

Mercure Airport Hotel Berlin Tegel

Kurt-Schumacher-Damm 202, 13405 Berlin
+49 30 41060
www.mercure.com

Situated to the east of the terminal area, near the motorway. Top floor rooms have views across some of the gates and runways. It is too distant for good photographs.

Berlin Schönefeld / Brandenburg

InterCityHotel Berlin Brandenburg

Am Seegraben 2, 12529 Berlin
+49 30 75657510
www.intercityhotel.com

This hotel has changed its name to reflect the new Brandenburg Airport which is opening to the south of the current airport site in the coming years, albeit after a length delay. However, the site of the hotel is actually opposite the Schönefeld Airport terminal. Rooms facing the airport can see some parking stands, and distant movements on the runway. It won't be as useful once the new airport is in full operation.

Bremen

Atlantic Hotel Bremen Airport

Flughafenallee 26, 28199 Bremen
+49 421 55710
www.atlantic-hotels.de

Linked to the terminal via a walkway. This hotel is only just taller than the terminal buildings, so a top floor room will have some views of aircraft on the taxiway and distant runway.

Holiday Inn Bremen Airport

Hanna-Kunath-Straße 5, 28199 Bremen
+49 421 322850
www.hiexpress.com

A brand new hotel. At present it faces an open car park, with the distant parking apron and runway beyond. You can't see much of the apron and aircraft will need to be identified with tracking websites or SBS.

Cologne/Bonn

Leonardo Hotel Cologne-Bonn Airport

Waldstrasse 255, Cologne 51147
+49 22 03 5610
www.leonardo-hotels.com

Conveniently located for the airport and motorway. Rooms can be expensive at times. The hotel is not ideally suited for viewing, although some upper rooms may offer views of the passenger apron and aircraft on finals to Runway 14R.

Dusseldorf

Sheraton Airport Hotel

Terminal-Ring 4, 40474 Düsseldorf
+49 21 14 1730
www.sheraton.com

The most convenient hotel at Düsseldorf Airport, and connected to the terminal via a walkway. Rooms on higher floors with numbers ending in 10 will give views of the domestic ramp and distant taxiway.

Frankfurt Hahn

B&B Hotel Frankfurt-Hahn Airport

Flugplatz Hahn, 55483 Hahn
+49 65 43 81800
www.hotelbb.de

Top floor rooms facing the airport look over the southern end of the passenger terminal. To the left there are views across the main taxiway to the runway.

Frankfurt Main

InterCity Hotel Frankfurt Airport

Am Luftbrückendenkmal 1, 60549 Frankfurt
+49 69 69 7099
www.intercityhotel.de

Located on the south side, close to the old USAF base. This hotel has some rooms offering limited views of the parallel runways. TV screens in the lobby often have aircraft registrations listed alongside movements. It is a short walk to the Autobahn Bridge spot.

Hilton Garden Inn

Am Flughafen, The Square – East, 60549 Frankfurt
+49 69 45 00 25 00
www.hilton.com

Situated near the terminals, above the railway station, this hotel also has TV screens in the lobbies with aircraft registrations (including the freighters) and some rooms with views of movements. There is an upgrade cost to book one of the quoted 'airport view' rooms. Useful to have flight tracking websites or equipment.

Park Inn by Radisson

Amelia-Mary-Earhart-Str. 10, Gateway Gardens, 60549 Frankfurt
+49 69 90 02 760
www.parkinn.com

This hotel is located a couple of minutes' walk from Terminal 2. Rooms on the 4th and 5th floors facing south have views of aircraft approaching runways 25L/C, and of aircraft departing 07C/R. You can also see runway 18 departures once they reach around 1,500ft.

Friedrichshafen

Hotel ibis Friedrichshafen Airport Messe

Am Flugpl. 72, 88046 Friedrichshafen
+49 7541 399070
www.ibis.com

A tall budget hotel between the convention centre and passenger terminal. Higher rooms have views over the parking apron and runway on one side, and the runway, museum and general aviation area on the other.

Hannover

Maritim Airport Hotel Hannover Airport

Flughafenstraße 5, 30669 Hannover
+49 511 97370
www.maritim.de

A tall hotel with various wings, linked to the passenger terminal. Top floor rooms facing south will have limited views of the aircraft gates and southern runway; those facing north have distant views of aircraft using the northern runway.

Munich

Holiday Inn Express

Freisiner Strasse 94, Schwaig, 85445
+49 81 22 95 880
www.hiexpress.com

Located in the village of Schwaig, a few miles from the airport. Rooms facing the airport can be requested. If traffic is landing over the hotel it is very low and easy to read off.

Greece

Athens

Sofitel Athens Airport

Athens Airport, Attiki Odos, Spata-Artemida 190 04
+30 21 0354 4000
www.sofitel.com

This eight-storey hotel is located right outside the airport terminal. Ask for a high room on floors 4-8 facing the airport and you won't miss many movements, which can be read off with binoculars. One side looks towards runway 03R/21L and the other 03L/21R; you can't see any aircraft parked at the terminal, however, and photography is not really possible.

Corfu

Corfu Holiday Palace Hotel

Corfu, 491 00
+30 2661 036540
corfuholidaypalace.gr

The best place to watch the action at Corfu is around the end of runway 35, where aircraft approach or depart over the sea. The Corfu Holiday Palace is a hotel with an elevated view over this end of the runway, so asking for a room with a view facing the lagoon should allow you to sit and watch the aircraft come and go from the comfort of your window all day.

Royal Boutique Hotel

Palaiopolis 110, 49100 Kanoni
+30 2661 035342
www.hotelroyal.gr

A little closer to the runway than the Holiday Palace, but with similar views of the action from an elevated position if you get a lagoon-facing room. Watch the aircraft from your balcony, with views down to the parking apron.

Heraklion

Aquis Arina Sand Hotel

Kokkini Hani, Gouves 715 00
+30 281 076 1293

This hotel is a little distant from the airport, along the coast to the east. However most aircraft approach from this direction and pass directly in front of the hotel around two miles from touchdown. As such you will see most movements, but they're too distant to photograph. It makes a good choice if you're holidaying on the island.

Rhodes

D'Andrea Mare Beach Hotel

Timokreontos, Rodos 851 01
+30 2241 096086

A resort hotel a mile or so to the east of the airport. Aircraft inbound to runway 25 pass very low over the hotel's pool and beach areas and can be read off easily.

Hotel Matoula Beach

Posidonos, Ialysos 851 00
+30 2241 094251

Like the D'Andrea (above), this hotel has great views of inbound arrivals to runway 25. In fact, it is a little closer to the airport than the D'Andrea.

Zakynthos

Golden Sun Hotel

Kalamákion, Каламакион 291 00
+30 2695 049074
goldensunhotels.com

A resort hotel close to Kalamaki Beach and the end of runway 34. Its position makes many rooms and their balconies, plus the pool area, perfect for low level spotting and photographs of aircraft approaching the airport from the south. Even departing traffic can be seen quite easily if the opposite runway direction is in use.

Hong Kong

Hong Kong Chek Lap Kok

Regal Airport Hotel

9 Cheong Tat Road, Hong Kong International Airport, Hong Kong
+825 2276 8888
www.regalhotel.com

This hotel is linked to the terminal building and some rooms have excellent views of aircraft. Be sure to ask for a room with views of the airport, and higher up if possible. The hotel is expensive, but is comfortable and has the benefit of the views and a restaurant which also overlooks the aprons and runways.

Marriott Skycity Hotel

1 SkyCity Road East, Hong Kong International Airport, Lantau Hong Kong
+852 3969 1888
www.marriott.com

Rooms in this hotel offer fantastic views, and it's only a short walk from the terminal and the Skydeck viewing area. Even numbered rooms high up offer views of short finals to runway 07R, and some views of the cargo ramp. Flight tracking software will be needed at night.

Iceland

Reykjavik

Icelandair Hotel Reykjavik Natura

Nauthólsvegur, Reykjavik
+354 444 4500
www.icelandairhotelreykjavik.com

A part of the old airport terminal, the Icelandair hotel is a good place for spotters visiting the city as one side of the hotel faces the airport's main runway and both of the main ramps. It's a good place to keep track of aircraft transiting the airport.

India

Chennai

Trident Hotel

1/24, G.S.T Road, Meenambakkam, Chennai, Tamil Nadu 600027
+91 44 2234 4747
www.tridenthotels.com

Some rooms at this hotel have views of the ends of runways 25 and 30, but the terminal area is not visible. The hotel's rooftop terrace is sometimes open, which also has views.

Delhi Indirha Gandhi Airport

Radisson Blu Plaza Delhi

Near Mahipalpur Extension, Nh 8, New Delhi, 110037
+91 11 2677 9191
www.radissonblue.com

Situated at the eastern side of the airport near the main motorway linking it to the city. This is a large and very comfortable and western hotel. Depending on your room you should be able to see aircraft arriving on runways 27, 28 and 29, and some departures. The terminals are a little far away, and higher rooms are better for seeing over the surrounding trees.

This is the hotel where a maid reported spotters for suspicious behaviour, leading to their arrest. So caution should be taken over your activities and leaving equipment such as binoculars, cameras and SBS units on display.

Hyderabad Airport

Novotel Hyderabad Airport

Rajiv Gandhi Airport, Hyderabad, Telangana 500409
+91 40 6625 0000
www.novotel.com

This hotel is located near the end of the runway at the eastern side of the airport. Rooms in the longer wing run parallel to the runway and can see departures towards the east, whilst those in the shorter wing facing toward the terminal, with brief views of aircraft on approach and departure. Always ask for the highest room possible.

Kolkata

Swissotel Kolkata

Plot No. 11/ City D Rajarhat East, 5 Mall Road, Newtown, Kolkata 700157
+91 33 6626 6666
www.swissotel.com

A little to the south of Kolkata Airport. If you can bag a floor in the Swiss Advantage range, which occupy the top three floors, you can get reasonable views across the airport and will see most movements.

Mumbai

Orchid Hotel

Adjacent to Domestic, 70-C, Nehru Rd, Vile Parle East, Mumbai, 400099
+91 22 2616 4040

A well-known hotel for spotters at Mumbai. It is found near Terminal 1 and the runway 14 threshold. Its roof terrace has a pool and good views over this part of the airport. Security, however, is now very tight and anyone using cameras or binoculars are usually spoken to immediately. Rooms on the top floor can have great views, with 702-707 reportedly good. Anyone with access to the executive floor can use the special lounge all day, which itself has good views. Spotting is allowed, but again no cameras.

Indesia

Jakarta Soekarno Hatta

Jakarta Airport Hotel

> *Terminal 2E, Soekarno-Hatta International Airport, Jakarta 19110*
> *+62 21 559 0008*
> *www.jakartaairporthotel.com*

This hotel is situated upstairs in the International Terminal and all rooms look out over the gates and northern runway. The corridor leading to the rooms has windows looking towards the domestic side of the airport and maintenance areas. Perfectly nice place to stay, but can be expensive and is often fully booked.

FM7 Resort Hotel

> *Jl. Raya Perancis No. 67, Benda, Kec. Tgr, Banten 15125*
> *+62 21 559 11777*
> *www.fm7hotel.com*

The FM7 Resort Hotel is situated close to the end of Runway 25R, and one of the main benefits is the proximity of aircraft approaching this runway, which can be photographed quite easily. Although the hotel is only two stories high, rooms on the top floor can be found that have good views and are not too obstructed by the surrounding trees. Some rooms also have views across to runway 25L, but SBS is necessary to identify them as they disappear behind the buildings. A rooftop Montezuma's Bar area also has views – this is open from 5am-1am, with an additional roof area open at the manager's discretion.

Surabaya Bandara International

Ibis Budget Hotel

Terminal 1, Jl. Ir. Juanda, Kec. Sidoarjo, 61253
+62 31 8688115
www.ibis.com

Set within Terminal 1 at Surabaya. Its rooms are above the terminal, and any facing the airport has a ramp and runway view, so you can spot and usually photograph as you wish. The hotel is basic, but comfortable.

Indonesia

Ireland

Dublin

Radisson Blu Dublin Airport

Dublin Airport
+353 1 844 6000
www.radissonblu.com

Rooms facing the airport have a distant view of movements at Dublin. If aircraft are arriving on runway 28, or using the new international pier, you should see them. Too distant for photography.

Italy

Genoa

MarinaPlace Hotel

Via Pionieri Ed Aviatori D'Italia, 129, 16154 Genova
+39 010 659401
www.marinaplace.it

This is an upmarket hotel which caters for the marina and many boats here. However, rooms facing the road look across the car park to the airport fence and runway just beyond. The hotel is only two storeys, but you should be able to see all movements.

Tower Genova Airport Hotel

Via Pionieri e Aviatori d'Italia, 44, 16154 Genova
+39 010 65491
www.towergenova.com

As its name suggests, this is a tall hotel. It sits alongside the parking ramp opposite the general aviation ramp. Rooms facing north look down on this ramp, with the passenger terminal and runway not quite visible to the left. Rooms facing south have a distant view of the runway and taxiway movements, and the top floors look down on the passenger terminal.

Rome Ciampino

Hotel Palacavicchi

Via di Ciampino, 70, 00178 Roma
+39 06 793 4210
www.hotelpalacavicchi.com

This hotel is only on one level, but rooms facing north are alongside the approach path to runway 15 less than a mile before touchdown, so are easy to read off. You can't see any of the airport, however.

Rome Fiumicino

Hilton Hotel Rome Airport

Via Arturo Ferrarin, 2, 00054 Fiumicino
+39 06 65258
www.hilton.com

Set amongst the car parks behind the terminal complex, and with good views over some of the aprons and the maintenance area. Distant views of movements on some of the runways can be had, but all is too far away for easy recognition or photography. The best rooms are even-numbered in the 004-012 range on the top floors.

Hilton Garden Inn Rome Airport

Via Vittorio Bragadin 2, 00054 Fiumicino, Italy
+39 06 6525 9000
www.hilton.com

Ask for an odd-numbered room on the 5th or 6th floors and you will have views of nearly all movements at the airport. Views are too distant for photography and SBS or flight tracking may be needed for registrations.

Japan

Nagoya Chubu Centrair

Centrair Hotel

1 Chrome-1 Centrair, Tokoname
+81 569 38 1111
www.centrairhotel.jp

The closest hotel to the airport terminal. It is a tall hotel, and upper rooms facing the airport have views of movements on the runway and domestic side of the terminal.

Osaka Kansai

Hotel Nikko Kansai Airport

Kansai Airport, Osaka 549-0001
+81 455 1111
www.nikkokix.com

Rooms on the top floor facing the airport have views of the taxiway, runways and part of the terminal.

Sapporo New Chitose

Air Terminal Hotel

New Chitose Airport
+81 123 45 6677
www.air-terminal-hotel.jp

Situated at the southern end of the passenger terminal. Directions are difficult, but once you find the place it is comfortable and perfect for a layover. One side of the hotel has rooms facing the parking apron and runways beyond, so is the best hotel option at the airport.

Tokyo Haneda

Haneda Excel Hotel Tokyo

3-4-2 Hanedakuko Ota, 144-0041 Tokyo
+81 3 5756 6000
www.tokyuhotelsjapan.com/en/

Linked to Terminal 2, this hotel offers some of the best views at the airport if you get the right room. Ask for a higher floor room facing the airport. It is quite expensive to stay at this hotel, but the location is superb. The observation decks at the terminals are only a short walk away.

Tokyo Narita

Marroad International Hotel

763-1 Komaino, Narita-shi, Chiba 286-0121
+81 476 30 2222
www.marroad.jp/narita/

Situated close to the threshold of runway 16R. If you ask for a room facing the airport, you will have views of this runway, the cargo apron and part of Terminal 1. Photographs are possible and most movements can be logged. The hotel's top-floor restaurant also has good views. Reasonably priced, with a free shuttle to the airport.

Narita Excel Tokyu Hotel

31 Oyama, Narita-shi, Chiba 286-0131
+81 476 33 0133
www.tokyuhotelsjapan.com/en/

Again, situated close to runway 16R and airport facing rooms have views of most movements. Photography is not good from here, however. A little more expensive than the Marroad, but worth it for seeing more movements and the arrivals screens in the lobby. Also has a free shuttle.

Luxembourg

Luxembourg Airport

NH Hotel Luxembourg Airport

Route de Treves, 1019 Luxembourg City
+352 34 05 71
www.nh-hotels.com

Some high floor rooms and the gym at this hotel face the Cargolux ramp at the eastern end of the airport, with a few also looking towards the terminal.

Macau

Macau Airport

Golden Crown China Hotel

Macau Airport
+853 2885 1166
www.htlchina.com.mo

A very tall hotel situated outside the terminal at Macau Airport. Higher rooms have a grandstand view over the action, and you can see aircraft coming to and from the terminal and movements on the distant runway.

Malaysia

Kuala Lumpur International Airport

Sama Sama Hotel

Jalan CTA 4 B, 64000 KLIA – Sepang, Selangor Darul Ehsan
+603 8787 3333
www.samasamahotels.com

Located alongside KLIA 1, making it close enough to walk to the viewing area. Rooms on the top floors and facing the airport allow most movements to be seen, although they can be a little distant for photography or reading off.

Tune Hotel

Lot Pt 13, Jalan KLIA 2/2 6400 KLIA, Selangor Darul Ehsan
www.tunehotels.com

A new hotel built alongside the KLIA 2 low-cost terminal and connected via a covered walkway. Some rooms on the sixth floor face the nearest runway and associated taxiway. No gates can be seen at either KLIA1 or 2. Rooms get free Wi-Fi.

Maldives

Male

Hotel Jen Male

Ameer Ahmed Magu, Male 20096
+960 330 0888
www.hoteljen.com

This hotel is in the city, on the island opposite the airport. As it is quite tall, some rooms on the top floors, as well as the rooftop terrace, have views towards the airport and final approach from both directions. Aircraft can clearly be seen with binoculars, but are too distant to read off registrations or photograph.

Mexico

Mexico City

Camino Real Hotel

Peñón de los Baño, Venustiano Carranza, Mexico City
+52 55 2482 2400
www.caminoreal.com

The best spotting hotel at Mexico City. Rooms on the 7th and 8th floors facing the airport are ideal, with movements on taxiways and runways visible, as well as some of the distant maintenance ramps.

Netherlands

Amsterdam Schiphol

Sheraton Amsterdam Airport

Schiphol Boulevard 101, Amsterdam Schiphol
+31 20 316 4300
www.sheraton.nl

Good for spotting most movements if you ask for a high room facing the airport. You will see aircraft parked at a number of the gates, along with taxiways and some of the runways. The hotel is a little too distant for photography. Can be expensive.

CitizenM Hotel

Jan plezierweg 2, 1118 BB Amsterdam Schiphol
+31 20 811 7080
www.citizenm.com

A modern, affordable hotel which is part of a popular chain. All rooms have double beds, and are very compact. Check-in is via a computer in the lobby, however staff can then make changes if you request them, such as a room overlooking the airport. Rooms on the 4th and 5th floor should be fine, and look out over the low-cost H pier, plus the runways and taxiways beyond. You shouldn't miss much if you use SBS or flight tracking website, but photography is not really possible.

New Zealand

Auckland International

Novotel Auckland Airport

Ray Emery drive, Auckland 2022
+64 9 257 7200
www.novotel.com

A relatively new hotel linked to the International Terminal. It is quite tall, so a room on one of the top floors will allow you to see over the terminal building. Only one side of the hotel has views of aircraft, and there are no views of the domestic or cargo aprons.

Norway

Bergen

Clarion Hotel Bergen Airport

Flyplassvegen 551, 5258 Blomsterdalen
+47 56 10 00 00
www.nordicchoicehotels.com

This hotel is in the car park at the northern end of the terminal and has rooms looking out onto the commuter ramp and some of the main gates. In the distance is the runway, so all movements should be visible if you have a room facing west on a high floor.

Oslo Gardermoen

Radisson Blu Airport Hotel Oslo

Hotelvegen, P.O. Box 163, N - 2061 Gardermoen
+47 63 93 30 00
www.radissonblu.com/hotel-osloairport

Quite expensive, but ideally located. Has many rooms higher up that have views of movements on runways 01L/19R. Hotel can usually accommodate your request.

Comfort Hotel RunWay

Hans Gaarders veg 27, Gardermoen 2060
+47 63 94 88 88
www.comfortinn.com

Situated next to the perimeter fence overlooking Runway 01L/19R. To get there from the airport you either take the dedicated S44 hotel shuttle bus at 70NOK or the cheaper normal service bus 855 which involves a short 2 minute walk from the stop to the hotel. Rooms facing the runway allow you to read off all movements, but tress can get in the way of photographs and views across to the terminal.

Stavanger Sola

Scandic Hotel Stavanger Airport

Flyplassvegen 226, 4055 Sola
+47 51 71 64 00
www.scandichotels.com

A new hotel at Stavanger, built into the terminal. High rooms offer views over some of the parking gates and taxiways. The hotel confirms that room 617 has the best views.

Philippines

Manilla

Belmont Hotel

Newport Boulevard Newport City, Pasay, 1301 Metro Manila
+63 2 855 7580
www.thebelmonthotels.com

A tall, ten-floor hotel with a rooftop pool and bar area. It is situated next to the International Terminal. The best rooms on the 10th floor are odd-numbered from 1027 to 1047, and offer views across the airport and nearer parking gates.

Remington Hotel

Newport Boulevard, Pasay 1309 Metro Manila
+63 2 908 8600
www.rwmanila.com

This hotel is excellent if you get a good room overlooking the airport. Generally rooms on the fifth floor upwards in the range xx009-xx0017 and xx0068-xx0073 will be perfect. Photography is possible from the rooms of aircraft on the nearby taxiway and runway. It is also next to the Air Force Museum.

Poland

Krakow

Hilton Garden Inn

Kapitana Mieczyslawa Medweckiego 3, Balice, 32-083
+48 12 3400000
www.hilton.com

A brand new hotel located just behind the terminal at Krakow Airport. Rooms at the front of the hotel overlook the parking apron for airliners. Other parts of the airport are obscured, however.

Warsaw

Courtyard Warsaw Airport

Żwirki i Wigury 1, 00-906 Warszawa
+48 22 650 01 00
www.marriott.com

A large, modern hotel outside the passenger terminal. The terminal buildings largely obstruct any views, but if you secure a top-floor room facing south you can see across to the runways and some of the gates at the southern end of the terminal.

Portugal

Lisbon

Radisson Blu Lisbon Airport

Avenida Marechal Craveiro Lopes 390, Lisbon 1749-009
+351 21 004 5000
www.radissonblu.com

The only hotel at Lisbon with any aircraft views. Situated a short distance south of the end of runway 03. Even-numbered rooms on the 10th floor yield the best results.

Qatar

Doha Hamad International

Oryx Rotana Hotel

Al Nahda School Street, Airport Road, Doha
+974 4402 3333
www.rotana.com

Although situated alongside the old Doha International Airport, or Oryx Rotana has views of both, albeit very distant of the new Hamad International. The old airport at present still sees some military and light aircraft movements. If you secure a room above the entrance on the top floors you should see movements at both airports.

Romania

Bucharest Otopeni

angelo Airporthotel Bucharest

Calea Bucureştilor 283, Otopeni 075100
+40 21 203 6500
www.angelo-bucharest.com

The position of this hotel on the access road to the airport, and between the two runways, means you can get good views of either the north or the south runway depending on which room you're in. Odd-numbered rooms 401-421 have views of arrivals on runway 08L, whilst even-numbered rooms 402-420 have views of 08R arrivals, and can see some movements at Baneasa Airport in the distance.

Russia

Moscow Domodedovo

Airhotel

> *Moskva 142015*
> *+7 495 795 38 68*
> *www.airhotel.ru*

The only hotel at the airport. It has rooms which have some views of the approach to the parallel runways 14L/R, but is not good for photography and you'll need to use SBS or flight tracking websites to tie them up.

Moscow Sheremetyevo

Hotel Novotel Moscow Sheremetyevo

> *Mezhdunarodnoye sh., Moskva, 141400*
> *+7 495 626 59 00*
> *www.novotel.com*

The closest hotel to the main terminal buildings. A room such as 6143 on the top floor has views of the runways in the distant, and aircraft parked at the terminal in the foreground. There is a lot of clutter in between, so photography is out of the question.

St Petersburg Pulkovo

Park Inn St Petersburg Airport

> *41 Pulkovskoye Shosse, 196140, St. Petersburg*
> *+7 812 640 55 00*
> *www.parkinn.com*

A new, tall hotel outside the modern Pulkovo-1 terminal. Rooms facing the terminal may have some views of aircraft movements, but those on a higher floor facing away have better views of some of the remote parking ramps and the old terminal.

Singapore

Singapore Changi

Crowne Plaza

75 Airport Boulevard #01-01, Singapore 819664
+65 6823 5354
www.crowneplaza.com

The best hotel for spotting at Singapore Changi, but expensive. Views from the even numbered rooms are excellent if you get one on floors 7, 8 or 9 facing the airport. You will have views of some Terminal 3 gates and the main runway. Corridors can also be used for views of the central terminal area.

Changi Village Hotel

1 Netheravon Road, Singapore 508502
+65 6379 7111
www.villagehotelchangi.com.sg

If you ask for a room facing the sea, you will be able to read off arriving aircraft landing on runway 20R and see aircraft using 20L, or 02L/R. An SBS is useful for night time movements. Again this is another fairly expensive hotel.

Sint Maarten

Princess Juliana International

Sonesta Maho Beach Hotel
1 Rhine Drive, Sint Maarten
+1 721 545 3100
www.sonesta.com/mahobeach

The natural choice for spotters. Situated alongside the beach, if you take a room facing the airport the aircraft will be at the same level (or lower) as your balcony, making it a great position for photography.

Sonesta Ocean Point Resort

Rhine Drive, Sint Maarten
+1 721 545 3100
www.sonesta.com/oceanpoint

A newer resort further along the cliff from the Sonesta Maho Beach. This one is an adult only hotel and also has views of aircraft passing low in front prior to landing over Maho Beach from nearly all of its suite rooms. The hotel's rooftop AZUL restaurant also has great views.

South Africa

Johannesburg O R Tambo International

Protea O R Tambo

Gladiator St, Kempton Park, 1619
+27 11 977 2600
www.proteahotels.com

The hotel of choice for spotters at Johannesburg. It is located opposite the passenger terminal and high rooms facing the airport look out over part of the parking apron and aircraft which day stop. You can also see runway 21R in the distance. Photography is possible of some movements with a long lens.

South Korea

Seoul Gimpo

Lotte City Hotel Gimpo Airport

38, Haneul-gil, Gangseo-gu, Seoul
+82 2 6116 1000
www.lottehotel.com

Some of the rooms at this modern hotel have great views over the terminal buildings to the parking aprons and runways beyond. A little too distant for photography, and you may need flight trackers for some aircraft. But the best option here by far.

Seoul Incheon

Grand Hyatt Incheon Hotel

208 Yeongjonghaeannam-ro, 321 Beon-gil, Unseo-dong, Jung-gu,
Incheon 400-719
+82 32 745 1234
incheon.grand.hyatt.com

Located close to the end of runway 33, rooms facing the airport have views of this. Aircraft are quite far, so need a good pair of binoculars to read off. The hotel is fairly expensive. There is a free shuttle bus to the terminal.

Best Western Premier Hotel Incheon Airport

48-27 Gonghang-ro 424beon-gil, Jung-gu, Incheon
+82 32 743 1000
www.airportshotel.co.kr/en

Located in a similar position to the Hyatt, it is a little more reasonable but offers views of runway 33L and some views of the terminals from some rooms on floors 9 and 10. In-room TVs have a channel listing arrivals and departures, including cargo and GA movements.

Spain

Fuerteventura

Barceló Fuerteventura Thalasso Spa

Avenida de El Castillo, s/n, 35610 Caleta de Fuste, Antigua, Las Palmas
+34 928 54 75 17
www.barcelo.com

One of a number of hotels in the Costa Caleta resort to the south of the airport. Aircraft on final approach pass directly overhead the airport and its pool area, and are easy to read off but too distant to photograph.

Lanzarote

Hotel Beatriz Playa

Puerto del Carmen, Las Palmas
+34 928 51 21 66
www.beatrizhoteles.com

A perfectly positioned hotel alongside the end of runway 03. Rooms facing Arrecife face the end of the runway, where aircraft on the ground and on approach can be seen and photographed. Rooms 3028-3050 are reportedly the best.

Sol Lanzarote Hotel

Calle Grama, 2, 35510 Puerto del Carmen, Las Palmas
+34 928 51 48 88
www.melia.com

The next resort along the coast from the Beatriz Playa. You can't see aircraft on the ground, but all aircraft on approach to runway 03 pass right by the hotel, visible from many rooms and the pool area.

Madrid Barajas

Express by Holiday Inn Madrid Airport

Avenida de Aragón 402, Madrid 28022
+34 917 48 16 57
www.hiexpress.com

Affordable hotel on the road to Torrejon Air Base. Rooms offer views of aircraft arriving on runway 33R, or (more distant) departures in the opposite direction. You can also see arrivals into Torrejon.

Palma de Mallorca

Hotel Marina Luz

Calle Maestro Ekitai Ahn 40, 07610 Cala Estancia, Mallorca
+34 971 49 24 00
www.marinaluzhotel.com/en

Probably the most popular hotel at Palma with spotters, located in Ca'n Pastilla. Its rooms have great views of aircraft on one of the runways, and is a short distance from the airport. Ask for a top-floor room facing the Bay of Palma for the best views. This is an adult-only hotel.

Tenerife South / Reina Sofia

Apartamentos Gema Aguamarina Golf

Av. del Atlàntico, 5, 38640 Golf del Sur, Santa Cruz de Tenerife
+34 922 73 83 17
www.adorahotels.com

Part of the golf resorts a couple of miles west of the airport. Rooms in the range x17-x32 on most floors will allow arrivals to be seen. The pool area is also good for watching arrivals. Photography at a distance is possible.

Aparthotel Cordial Golf Plaza

Avenida J.M. Galván Bello, 38639, Golf del Sur, Santa Cruz de Tenerife
+34 922 73 70 00
www.cordialcanarias.com

The pool area at this hotel is great for watching arrivals from the west onto runway 08, about a mile before touchdown. Rooms 131-138 and 230-236 are also good for watching aircraft.

Valencia

Travelodge Valencia Aeropuerto

C/ Las Rosas, 31, 46940 Manises
+34 961 52 39 30
www.travelodge.es

Only the top two floors give any views from this hotel. They look out over the domestic parking ramp and the runway, with rooms 605 and 607 reportedly the best. If you're on a different floor you can walk to see movements from the corridors on the top floors.

Sweden

Gothenburg Landvetter

Landvetter Airport Hotel

Flygets Hotellväg, 438 13 Landvetter
+46 31 97 75 50
www.landvetterairporthotel.com

This hotel is set among the car parks behind the terminal. The views are not perfect, but you can see movements on the runway from a distance over the terminal buildings.

Stockholm Bromma

Mornington Hotel

Norrbyvägen 30, 168 69 Stockholm-Bromma
+46 8 507 332 00
www.mornington.se

Less than a mile from the end of runway 30, directly under the flightpath for arriving and departing traffic. Not perfect for photography and you may need to go outside to properly identify aircraft. But you should see all movements, even light aircraft.

Stockholm Arlanda

Radisson Blu Sky City Hotel

Stockholm Arlanda Airport, SE-190 45
+46 8 506 740 00
www.radissonblu.com

Located above the terminals and linked into the Sky City area. Rooms higher up and at each end of the building offer great views over the movements – particularly of Runway 01L/19R. Photography is not really possible, however. The hotel can be expensive.

Jumbo Stay Hostel

Jumbovägen 4, 190 47 Stockholm Arlanda
+46 8 593 604 00
www.jumbostay.se

A unique high-end hostel inside a former Pan Am Boeing 747-200 (last registration 3D-NEE). It is situated just off the airport link road, close to the cargo terminal and a taxiway. Rooms are comfortable and most have views of some movements, but photography is not possible. Wi-Fi internet is free of charge.

Switzerland

Bern

Airport Hotel-Restaurant

Flugplatzstrasse 57, 3123 Belp
+41 31 961 61 81
www.airhotel.ch

A small hotel at a small airport. But nevertheless, rooms face the parking ramp and runway and you can see all movements at fairly close quarters.

Geneva

NH Geneva Airport Hotel

Av. De Mategnin 21, Geneva 1217
+41 22 989 9999
www.nh-hotels.com

One of the best-placed hotels at Geneva Airport for the enthusiast. Although only Superior rooms offer views, the ones that do face the threshold of Runway 05. The hotel is also close to the spotting location at this end of the runway.

Zurich

Park Inn Zurich Airport

Flughofstrasse 75, 8153 Rümlang
+41 44 828 8686
www.parkinn.com

If you request a room overlooking the airport, you won't be disappointed. Most of the action is visible from here, although photography is a little limited due to the distance and glass. This hotel can be fairly expensive.

Taiwan

Tapiei Taoyuan

Hotel Novotel Taipei Taoyuan Airport

1-1 Terminal South Road, Taoyuan County, Dayuan Township, 337 Taipei
+886 3398 0888
www.novotel.com

The closest hotel to the airport, and situated between the two runways alongside the roads which lead to the terminals. Even numbered rooms on floors 7, 8 and 9 face either towards runway 05 or 06 thresholds, and as such you can get views of many (but not all) movements depending on the direction in use.

Thailand

Bangkok Don Mueang

Amari Hotel Don Mueang

333 Chert Wudthakas Road, Si Kan, Don Mueang, Bangkok 10210
+66 2 566 1020
www.amari.com/donmuang/

This hotel is connected to the terminals via a walkway. Rooms on floors 4 and above have views of aircraft once they have departed from runways 21L/R, or whilst on final approach. They can not be seen on the ground.

Bangkok Suvarnabhumi

Phoenix Hotel

88 Ladkrabang 7, Ladkrabang Road, Bangkok 10520
+66 2 737 1446
www.phoenixhotelbangkok.com

The best-known hotel for spotting at Suvarnabhumi airport. Management understand the needs of spotters and will grant access to the rooftop area and balcony facing final approach to runway 19R. The hotel is only 2 miles from the terminal and very affordable. Ask staff and they can provide you with a list of the day's arrivals.

Grand Inn Come Hotel

99 Moo 6 Kingkaew Road, Rachathewa, Bangkok 10540
+66 2 738 8191
www.grandinncome-hotel.com

A basic but pleasant hotel situated alongside the airport perimeter to the west. Top floor rooms overlook runway 19R/01L, with 541 reported as having great views. Most movements can be seen and tied up with SBS or flight tracker websites. Photography is possible if you have a long lens and can cope with the heat haze.

Phuket

Centara Grand West Sands Resort

Soi Mai Khao 4, Mai Khao, Thalang District, Phuket 83110
+66 76 372 000
www.centarahotelsresorts.com

A family resort hotel located close to Phuket Airport with great amenities and nearby beach. Some rooms have balconies and views of the airport apron and runway approach. Jonathan Payne, the Executive Assistant Manager, is keen to accommodate the needs of spotters. Call ahead to make a request for a room with the best views.

Turkey

Antalya

Lara Hotel

Güzeloba Mh., Antalya
+90 242 349 2930
www.larakaprisotel.com

Away from the tourist resort hotels, the Lara is still a comfortable and affordable place to stay on the cliffs to the south of the airport. All rooms face the sea, with balconies, and aircraft approaching can be seen on either side, depending on the runway in use. Additionally, the pool area is also a good place to watch aircraft, but you may need to use an SBS to tie up some – especially if departing over the hotel towards the sea.

Istanbul Ataturk

Radisson Blu Airport Hotel

E-5 Karayolu (Yanyol) No. 20 - Sefakoy Kavsagi - K. Cekmece - 34295 Istanbul
+90 212 411 3838
www.radissonblu.com

A perfect place to stay if you can get a room overlooking the airport. You'll be able to see all movements on the 18L/36R runway, and many around the terminal area, plus the GA area.

WOW Airport Hotel

34149 Istanbul
+90 212 468 3000
www.wowhotelsistanbul.com

An alternative to the Radisson. It has two towers, one 5-star and the other 4-star. The lower quality has great views across the parallel runways from top floor rooms facing the airport. You have a brief view of traffic on the other runway, and can also see across the storage area from the corridor windows. Room 1715 reportedly good.

United Arab Emirates

Dubai International

Sheraton Deira Hotel

Al Muteena St, Dubai, United Arab Emirates
+971 4 268 8888
www.sheratondeiradubai.com

For most spotters visiting Dubai, this is the only place to consider for watching aircraft. The Sheraton Deira is a very comfortable (albeit quite pricey) hotel, but its rooftop pool area sits underneath the approach/departure path to Dubai's runways and aircraft pass fairly low overhead throughout the day and night. Aircraft approaching are within reach of a decent camera lens, and hotel staff are understanding of the hobby provided spotters don't upset other guests or make equipment visible to the street below. The elevation of the rooftop area also means the airport is in clear view, although the heat haze can make it difficult to see clearly.

Nojoum Hotel Apartments

Abubaker Al Siddique Road, Dubai, United Arab Emirates
+971 4 265 8888
www.nojoumsuites.com

The Nojoum has rooms facing the approach to the airport at a more side-on angle than the Sheraton Deira. Ask for a room on at least the fifth floor for the best views. Rooms have balconies, which are useful for private spotting without worrying about equipment. The hotel does, however, also have a similar rooftop pool area which can be used for spotting.

United Kingdom

Aberdeen

Holiday Inn Express

3, International Ave, Dyce, Aberdeen AB21 0BE
+44 1224 608300
www.hiexpress.com

This is a new hotel built to the south of the terminal, close to other hotels but it seems it has the best views of all of them. Ask for a room facing the runway for views of aircraft movements and helicopter operations.

Birmingham

Travelodge Birmingham Airport

Terminal Road, Birmingham B26 3QW
+44 871 984 6483
www.travelodge.co.uk

Located on the old terminal side of the airport, rooms facing the airport on the top two floors have great views across the runway and to the passenger terminal. You can't see the executive and cargo ramp, but will see all movements.

Doncaster Sheffield

Ramada Encore Doncaster Airport

First Ave, Doncaster DN9 3GP
+44 1302 718520
www.ramada.co.uk

Situated in behind the car park near the airport terminal. Rooms facing the terminal can see some of the gates and the runway beyond, so no movements should be missed.

East Midlands

Radisson Blu East Midlands

Pegasus Business Park, Herald Way, East Midlands Airport DE74 2TZ
+44 1509 67055
www.radissonblu.co.uk

A recent addition. Many rooms overlook the threshold of runway 27 and parts of the eastern cargo ramp. You can see most movements, and photograph aircraft arriving/departing with a 300mm lens.

Edinburgh

Travelodge Edinburgh Airport

Ratho Park, Glasgow Rd, Edinburgh EH28 8PP
0871 984 6340
www.travelodge.com

Ask for a room overlooking the A8/Glasgow Road. These face the threshold of runway 06, giving you views of most movements. It would be beneficial to be on the top floor as trees outside the hotel can obscure the view.

Liverpool John Lennon

Hampton by Hilton Liverpool Airport

Speke Hall Ave, Liverpool L24 1YD
0845 122 6787
www.hilton.com

Set in the car park outside the terminal. This is quite a tall hotel, so rooms on either side on the top floors have fleeting views of aircraft on the ground, and using the runway beyond.

Crowne Plaza Liverpool Airport

Liverpool, Merseyside, L24 8QD
+44 151 494 5000
www.crowneplaza.com

This is an interesting hotel in that it occupies the former passenger terminal at the original Liverpool Speke Airport, a little to the west of the current airport. The fantastic art deco building has been preserved well, and rooms facing south look out on the former apron where there is a collection of historic airliners under preservation. You may also have distant views of aircraft approaching runway 09 or departing 27.

London City

London City Airport Travelodge

Hartmann Road, Silvertown, London E16 2BZ
0871 984 6333
www.travelodge.co.uk

A short distance from the terminal and on the main access road. Higher rooms facing north have a view over the end of runway 09 and the biz jet ramp. The best ones are 503 to 509. You shouldn't miss too many movements from here. Please note that these are family rooms, so you'll need to request one when booking.

London Gatwick

BLOC Hotel

South Terminal Gatwick Airport, RH6 0NP
+44 20 3051 0101
www.blochotels.com

Situated atop the South Terminal in the former administration building, the BLOC Hotel is a great place to spot if you have a room facing the airport. It has similar views to the old viewing terrace. Depending on the room you will usually have a view of both terminals and part of the runway.

Sofitel London Gatwick Airport

North Terminal, Gatwick Airport RH6 0PH
+44 1293 567070
www.sofitel.com

Smart hotel situated at the North Terminal, and linked via monorail from the South Terminal. Rooms on the higher floors facing the airport have unrivalled views of aircraft movements to both terminals.

London Heathrow

Renaissance London Heathrow

140 Bath Road, Hounslow TW6 2AQ
+44 20 88 97 63 63
www.marriott.com

This is one of the best spotting hotels in the world, if you request a room overlooking the airport. All movements on the northern runway can be read off and photographed easily. Movements around the terminals are easy to spot. Those using SBS can continue to spot throughout the night. Although this hotel is not the cheapest at Heathrow, the quality of spotting makes up for it and it offers special spotter packages through its website.

Hilton Garden Inn London Heathrow

Eastern Perimeter Rd, Hounslow, TW6 2SQ
+44 20 8266 4664
www.hilton.com

Formerly the Jury's Inn. There are rooms which face south, overlooking aircraft on short final to runway 27L, or north/west which look out over part of the airport and the northerly runway. Choose which you'd prefer and make a request.

Holiday Inn London Heathrow Ariel

118 Bath Road, Harlington, Hayes UB3 5AJ
+44 20 89 90 00 00
www.holidayinn.com

Another good spotting hotel at Heathrow. Even-numbered rooms between 270 and 284 have the best views of aircraft using the northern runway and terminal areas. Photography is possible. The hotel is more affordable than the Renaissance.

Ibis London Heathrow

112 Bath Rd, Hayes, London UB3 5AL
+44 20 8759 4888
www.ibis.com

A little further east than the Ariel. Odd-numbered rooms on the top floor are great for watching and photographing arrivals on runway 27R. You can't see much on the ground, but it is a short walk to the perimeter road.

Thistle London Heathrow

Bath Rd, Longford, London UB7 0EQ
0871 376 9021
www.thistle.com

A good option if aircraft are landing on runway 09L from the west. This hotel is opposite the threshold of this runway, close to Terminal 5. Few rooms have views, but you might get lucky if you ask. There is a terrace you can use which has good views.

London Luton

Holiday Inn Express Luton Airport

2 Percival Way, Luton LU2 9GP
+44 1582 589100
www.hiexpress.com

Rooms facing the airport are all great for logging aircraft on the runway and some taxiways, and also have plenty of opportunities for good photographs.

London Southend

Holiday Inn Southend Airport

77 Eastwoodbury Cres, Southend-on-Sea SS2 6XG
+44 1702 543001
www.holidayinn.com

This hotel's location is perfectly suited for in-room spotting. All rooms on the north side of the building (including Standard, Executive, and King Superior rooms) face towards the runway and terminal ramp. The rooftop restaurant and bar also has panoramic views.

London Stansted

Radisson Blu London Stansted Airport

Waltham Close, Stansted Airport, Essex CM24 1PP
+44 1279 661012
www.radissonblue.co.uk

A very smart, modern hotel at Stansted with prices at the higher end. Some higher rooms facing the airport have views over the Ryanair pier and Runway 23 threshold. The hotel is only a few metres from the Terminal.

Manchester

Radisson Blu Manchester Airport

Chicago Avenue, Manchester M90 3RA
+44 161 490 5000
www.radissonblu.co.uk

The best hotel for spotting at Manchester. Located behind Terminal 2, rooms on high floors overlook the aprons and the runways in the distance. The restaurant also offers the same view. Some good opportunities for photographs with a long lens. The hotel is rarely cheap.

Newcastle

Premier Inn Newcastle Airport

Ponteland Rd, Newcastle upon Tyne NE20 9BX
0871 527 8796
www.premierinn.com

Rooms facing south have a view of aircraft approaching runway 07, or departing runway 25. They also have a slight view of some of the parking gates.

Southampton

Premier Inn Southampton Airport

Mitchell Way, Southampton SO18 2XU
0871 527 8998
www.premierinn.com

It's possible to get fleeting views of the runway, and of part of the terminal parking apron, from this modern hotel just to the south of the terminal. Ask for a room facing the car park.

United States

Alaska

Anchorage Ted Stevens International / Lake Hood Seaplane Base

Lake Hood Inn

4702 Lake Spenard Drive, Anchorage, AK 99509
+1 907 258 9321
www.lakehoodinn.com

This small hotel only has four bedrooms, but the whole place is aviation themed, with pictures, aircraft models and parts on display. The Bravo bedroom is the best for views over the movements at Lake Hood Seaplane Base, and distant arrivals at the main airport.

Microtel Inn & Suites by Wyndham Anchorage Airport

5205 Northwood Dr, Anchorage, AK 99517
+1 907 245 5002
www.microtelinn.com

This hotel is just north of the main road linking the city to the airport. Room facing south look out onto the approach path to the east/west runways, so you can monitor and movements on these runways from a distance. You need to be above ground floor due to the trees outside the hotel.

Fairbanks Airports

Pike's Waterfront Lodge

1850 Hoselton Rd, Fairbanks, AK 99709
+1 877 774 2400
www.pikeslodge.com

Sandwiched between the Chena River and Airport Way, Pike's Waterfront Lodge is an affordable place to stay. Rooms facing the road look across to the approach path to runways 20L/R, so you can monitor movements if they are from this direction. A short walk in front of the hotel leads to a good place to watch and photograph these arrivals.

Juneau Airport

Extended Stay America

1800 Shell Simmons Dr, Juneau, AK 99801
+1 907 790 6435
www.extendedstayamerica.com

A budget hotel just north of the terminal. Rooms facing south can see the parking aprons and runway beyond through gaps in the trees.

Arizona

Phoenix Sky Harbor

Aloft Hotel

4450 East Washington, Phoenix, AZ 85034
+1 602 275 6300
www.aloftphoenixairport.com

North of the airport. Rooms facing the front of the hotel look out towards the approach to runway 26, which you can read off with binoculars.

Crowne Plaza

4300 East Washington Ave, Phoenix, AZ 85034
+1 602 273 7778
www.crowneplazaphx.com

Situated close to the Aloft Hotel. Even-numbered rooms on high floors offer views of the airport's north side. You can read off aircraft quite easily with good binoculars.

Tucson Airport

Four Points by Sheraton Tucson Airport

7060 S Tucson Blvd, Tucson, AZ 85756
+1 520 746 0271
www.starwoodhotels.com

Not ideal, but the best of the bunch at Tucson. The Four Points is close to the airport entrance, near the terminal. If you can get on the top floor, facing the airport, you can see most airliner movements in between buildings and other obscructions.

Arkansas

Little Rock National

Comfort Inn & Suites Airport

4301 E Roosevelt Rd, Little Rock, AR 72206
+1 501 376 2466
www.airporthotellittlerock.com

A small budget chain hotel situated off the entrance road to the terminal area. Rooms facing north above ground floor look across to runway 4L/22R and you can see some other movements around the airport at a distance.

California

Oakland Airport

Holiday Inn Express & Suites Oakland – Airport

66 Airport Access Rd, Oakland, CA 94603
+1 510 569 4400
www.oaklandhiexpress.com

Hotels at Oakland are situated near the airport entrance, at the northern part of the site. The Holiday Inn Express offers the best views if you get a top floor room facing the road and airport, however the passenger terminal is a long way off. You will be able to see movements on the northern runways, which is mainly light and executive aircraft. You will also see the FedEx Express ramp from a distance.

LA/Ontario Airport

Embassy Suites Ontario Airport

3663 E Guasti Rd, Ontario, CA 91761
+1 909 605 0281
www.hilton.com

This hotel is set back to the north east of the airport, but its height means that rooms on the top floors facing south look out onto the final approach from the east, or departures from the west. It is too distant to see aircraft on the ground, but with a flight tracker you should get most movements.

Long Beach

Holiday Inn Long Beach Airport

2640 N Lakewood Blvd, Long Beach, CA 90815
+1 562 597 4401
www.hilongbeach.com

This hotel and conference center is at the southern end of the airport, on the opposite side of the runway to the Marriott (see below). It has a tall, circular block of rooms, so ask for one facing the airport and you will see movements on the runway, and some other parts of the airport.

Long Beach Marriott

4700 Airport Plaza Dr, Long Beach, CA 90815
+1 562 425 5210
www.marriott.com

Situated alongside the runway and N Lakewood Blvd at the south eastern corner of the airport. This hotel is fairly tall, so rooms on higher floors facing the airport will have a view of movements on the main runway, particularly when arriving from the south. Distant views of other parts of the airport may be possible.

Los Angeles LAX

Crowne Plaza

5985 Century Blvd, Los Angeles, CA 90045
+1 310 642 7500
www.crowneplaza.com

This tall hotel to the east of the terminals has views over the southern airport and runways and cargo area. Ask for a room facing the airport and you'll be able to log registrations easy. It is not a great hotel for photography. The hotel's multi-storey car park also has good views.

Four Points by Sheraton

9750 Airport Blvd, Los Angeles, CA 90045
+1 310 645 4600
www.fourpointslax.com

Situated closer to the terminals, this hotel has rooms facing either north or south. Unfortunately you can only have one or the other, so choose wisely and ask the friendly staff. Again, the rooms are not ideal for photography, but are perfect for logging aircraft. Can be quite cheap at weekends.

Embassy Suites LAX South

1440 E Imperial Ave, El Segundo, CA 92045
+1 310 640 3600
www.hilton.com

A favourite at LAX. Rooms on the 5th (top) floor looking towards the southern runways and nearby cargo and biz jet aprons can be requested. Photography can be difficult due to obstructions outside, but viewing is fine. You'll need tracking software for aircraft visible on the northern runways. Suites 580 and 581 are reportedly good, but a new building partially obscures views of the biz jet ramp. It's a short walk to Imperial Hill from here.

San Diego

Motel 6 San Diego Airport/Harbor

2353 Pacific Highway, San Diego, CA 92101
+1 619 232 8931
www.motel6.com

Ideally situated close to the official spotting location on Laurel Street, and underneath the final approach path to runway 27. Few rooms have views of aircraft, but most surrounding streets do.

San Francisco International

Marriott San Francisco Waterfront Airport

1800 Old Bayshore, Burlingame, CA 94010
+1 650 692 9100
www.marriott.com

The best-known hotel for spotting at SFO, with higher rooms facing the airport offer views over runways 1L/R and 28L/R.

Westin San Francisco Airport Hotel

1 Old Bayshore Highway, Millbrae, CA 94030
+1 650 692 3500
www.westinsanfranciscoairport.com

Next door to the Marriott, so a good alternative. Rooms facing the airport have views of part of the terminals, as well as the runways.

Santa Maria Airport

Radisson Hotel

3455 Skyway Dr, Santa Maria, CA 93455
+1 805 928 8000
www.radisson.com

One side of this hotel fronts onto the southern parking apron of the airport, where light aircraft generally park. Just beyond is the runway. So a room on this side will offer views of all movements at close hand.

Van Nuys Airport

Airtel Plaza Hotel

7277 Valjean Ave, Van Nuys, CA 91406
+1 818 997 7676
www.airtelplaza.com

The more expensive 'terrace' rooms at this hotel have a nice viewing balcony which overlooks the airport. Make sure you specify this is the view you want, as some may face other directions.

Colorado

Denver Centennial Airport

Ramada Englewood Hotel and Suites

7770 S Peoria St, Englewood, CO 80112
+1 303 790 7770
www.ramada.com

Ask for a top floor room facing south and you will have some views in-between the hangars of the east-west runway and one or two parking areas.

Denver International

Westin Denver Airport

8300 Peña Blvd, Denver, CO 80249
+1 303 317 1800
www.westindenverairport.com

A new hotel near the main terminal building. High floor rooms at either end of the building look out over the nearer parking stands and runways, and you can see movements elsewhere at a distance. This is a large airport, so it's hard to catch everything.

Connecticut

Hartford Bradley International

Candlewood Suites

149 Ella Grasso Turnpike, Windsor Locks, CT 06096
+1 860 623 2000
www.ihg.com

The car park of this hotel is underneath the approach to runway 33, with aircraft passing overhead very shortly before touchdown. Rooms facing this direction have a view of all approaching aircraft from the south. You can see part of the terminal in the distance.

SpringHill Suites Hartford Airport/Windsor Locks

225 Ella Grasso Turnpike, Windsor Locks, CT 06096
+1 860 758 7000
www.marriott.com

A roadside hotel which is part of the Marriott family. Rooms facing south look out towards the final approach to runway 33, and have distant views across to the terminal area.

Florida

Daytona Beach

Residence Inn Daytona Beach Speedway/Airport

1725 Richard Petty Blvd, Daytona Beach, FL 32114
+1 386 252 3949
www.marriott.com

Situated at the northern end of the airport, some rooms look out over the approach to runway 16 and can see some of the parking ramps for light aircraft. Most large aircraft use the main runway 07L/25R however.

Fort Lauderdale Hollywood

Sheraton Fort Lauderdale Airport & Cruise Port

1825 Griffin Road, Dania, FL 33004
+1 954 920 3500
www.starwoodhotels.com

This hotel has some rooms facing the approach to the airport. You won't see many airliner movements easily, but a SBS should help. It looks towards the southern runway.

Key West

Best Western Key Ambassador Resort Inn

3755 S Roosevelt Blvd, Key West, FL 33040
+1 305 296 3500
www.keyambassador.com

Most guests at this hotel would want rooms facing the pool and sea. However, rooms facing north are directly under the final stages of approach to Key West Airport's runway 27. Standing in the car park outside your room would be a perfect place for photographing aircraft landing here.

Miami International

Hilton Miami Airport

5101 Blue Lagoon Drive, Miami, FL 33126
+1 305 262 1000
www.hilton.com

A good hotel for views over the southern half of the airport, particularly when runways 27 or 30 are in use. Aircraft on the northern runways are a little difficult to see. Ask for a high room facing the airport. Executive double rooms with balconies offer the best views.

Comfort Inn & Suites

5301 NW 36th St, Miami Springs, FL 33166
+1 305 871 6000
www.comfortinn.com

The best hotel for in-room spotting at Miami. High rooms facing the airport overlook the 08/26 runways and northern airport. All movements can be seen, but those on the southern part of the airport may need a SBS or flight tracking site to tie up.

Miami Executive – Kendall/Tamiami

Holiday Inn Express & Suites Miami-Kendall

13475 SW 131st St, Miami, FL 33186
+1 786 837 2100
www.ihg.com

Although this hotel is a little way to the east of the airport, on the road leading in, you have views from rooms facing west of aircraft approaching this busy executive airport. Views of aircraft on the ground are not really possible, however.

Orlando International

Holiday Inn Express Orlando Airport

7900 S Conway Road, Orlando, FL 32812
+1 407 581 7900
www.hiexpress.com

This hotel has excellent views over the airport from the top floor. You will see most movements, and those on the nearby runways will be within range of decent cameras. Movements on the far runway can be tied up if you use flight tracking websites or SBS.

Hyatt Regency

9300 Jeff Fuqua Blvd, Orlando, FL 32827
+1 407 825 1234
www.orlandoairport.hyatt.com

By far the best hotel at Orlando Airport, and situated within the terminal complex. If you ask for a room facing the runways, you will see most movements. The hotel's car park and pool area also have views of movements.

Pensacola Regional

Hyatt Place Pensacola Airport

161 Airport Ln, Pensacola, FL 32504
+1 850 483 5599
www.hyatt.com

A medium-sized hotel set in the airport car park behind the terminal building. Rooms on the top floor facing the airport have partial views of the ramp and runways.

Tampa Airport

Renaissance Tampa International Plaza

4200 Jim Walter Blvd, Tampa, FL 33607
+1 813 877 9200
www.renaissance.com

Part of the large International Plaza mall and retail complex to the south of Tampa Airport. This hotel is tall, and rooms facing north, east or west have views over the southern part of the airport, albeit a little distant for photography.

Tampa Airport Marriott

4200 George J Bean Pkwy, Tampa, FL 33607
+1 813 879 5151
www.marriott.com

A large hotel at the northern end of the central terminal complex at Tampa. Rooms are spread over three wings, each facing different directions, so what you end up seeing may differ depending on where you are, since there are runways and terminals on either side of the hotel. A higher room is important nevertheless.

Georgia

Atlanta Hartsfield Jackson

Renaissance Concourse Hotel Atlanta Airport

1 Hartsfield Center Parkway, Atlanta, GA 30354
+1 404 209 9999
www.marriott.com

Many rooms at this fairly luxurious hotel overlook the entire airport, and many have private balconies, which give spotters the chance to spend all day and night watching the action. Aircraft on the furthest runways can be seen with good pole; everything else with a good pair of binoculars. Photography is possible on the closer runways too. The hotel offers spotter packages on request. It is cheaper at weekends. Rooms on higher floors are better, with 819, 933, 1016, 1022, 1024 and 1025 singled out as excellent.

Hawaii

Honolulu International

Best Western Plaza

3253 N Nimitz Hwy, Honolulu, HI 96819-1907
+1 808 836 3636
www.bestwesternhawaii.com

Located very close to the airport terminals, this hotel is quite tall and has views of movements on the nearest runways, and also certain ramps from rooms on the upper floors. Ask for an airport-facing room.

Illinois

Chicago Midway

Courtyard Midway Airport

6610 South Cicero Avenue, Chicago, IL 60638
+1 708 5633 0200
www.marriott.com

Many high level rooms look over the airport, and are available on request. It is possible to watch movements and note registrations, although photography is not worthwhile.

Chicago O'Hare

Hilton Chicago O'Hare

O'Hare International Airport, Chicago, Illinois 60666
+1 773 686 8000
www.hilton.com

Perfectly situated within Terminal 2 at the heart of O'Hare, this Hilton has rooms overlooking the American Airlines gates and southern runways. Ask for an even-numbered, high-floor room. Good photographs are possible of aircraft around the terminal. Unfortunately the hotel is quite expensive, and has started charging a premium for a guaranteed airport view room.

Quad City International / Moline

Motel 6

6920 27th St, Moline, IL 61265
+1 309 762 1711
www.motel6.com

Budget hotel alongside Route 6. It only has two floors, but an upstairs room facing the airport looks out across the airport at a distance. All three runways cross within view, so with the help of flight tracking you should catch most movements.

Quality Inn & Suites Moline - Quad Cities

6910 27th St, Moline, IL 61265
+1 309 517 6283
www.choicehotels.com

Situated next door to the Motel 6. It is slightly further back, but also slightly more elevated. Views from a distance across the airport.

Indiana

Indianapolis Airport

Radisson Hotel Indianapolis Airport

2500 S High School Rd, Indianapolis, IN 46241
+1 317 244 3361
www.radisson.com

This hotel was very convenient for the original passenger terminal at Indianapolis, which has now been demolished. Nevertheless, its higher rooms facing the airport have a good view over the airfield towards the distant new terminal and FedEx facility. You'll likely need SBS to tie up most of what you see, but you shouldn't miss too many movements.

Iowa

Des Moines

Hampton Inn Des Moines Airport

5001 Fleur Dr, Des Moines, IA 50321
+1 515 287 7300
www.hilton.com

There are a few hotels close together here, including a Motel 6, Days Inn and Quality Inn. However, the Hampton Inn seems to offer the best all-round views. It is possible watch aircraft arriving and departing on runway 23 at fairly close quarters, with some distant views of aircraft on the ground.

Holiday Inn Des Moines-Airport/Conference Center

6111 Fleur Dr, Des Moines, IA 50321
+1 515 287 2400
www.ihg.com

Along the same road as the Hampton Inn, but this time at the southern end of the airport. Rooms on the second floor facing the airport are good for views of aircraft arriving and departing on runway 31. You can also see a few of the terminal gates and the UPS ramp in the distance.

Kansas

Wichita

Double Tree by Hilton Wichita Airport

2098 Airport Road, Wichita, KS 67209
+1 316 945 5272
www.hilton.com

The best views from this hotel are in rooms facing west, which look out towards the cargo ramp. Some movements on the main runway 01L/19R can also be seen at a distance.

Kentucky

Louisville

Crowne Plaza Louisville Airport Expo Center

830 Phillips Ln, Louisville KY 40209
+1 502 367 2251
www.ihg.com

A short distance north of the passenger terminal. High level rooms facing the airport have views of movements on both runways. Photography is not possible, and during the night time UPS rush you will need SBS or flight tracking websites to tie up movements.

Louisiana

New Orleans Airport

Hilton New Orleans Airport

901 Airline Dr, Kenner, LA 70062
+1 504 469 5000
www.hilton.com

Probably the only hotel with any kind of view close to New Orleans Airport. This Hilton is located just south of the terminals, with higher rooms facing north looking out towards the airport. Sadly the concourse in front of you is no longer used, but you can see aircraft using the nearer north-south runway.

Maine

Bangor Airport

Four Points by Sheraton Bangor Airport

308 Godfrey Blvd, Bangor, ME 04401
+1 207 947 6721
www.fourpointsbangorairport.com

This tall hotel is linked to the terminal building. Ask for a high room facing the runway and you'll have a good view over all of the movements, including airliners, light aircraft and even the Air National Guard Boeing 707s.

Portland Airport

Embassy Suites by Hilton Portland Maine

1050 Westbrook St, Portland, ME 04102
+1 207 775 2200
www.hilton.com

This is the slightly better of the two hotels at Portland Airport (the other being the Hilton Garden Inn) on overall views. Ask for a high level room facing the airport. Although only the secondary runway is in view, you have a better view over the cargo, general aviation and executive ramps. Any airliner traffic can be seen in the distance using the main runway and tied up with a flight tracker.

Massachusetts

Boston Logan

Hilton Boston Logan

One Hotel Drive, Boston, MA 02128
+1 617 568 6700
www.hilton.com

The closest hotel to the terminal, and connected via a bridge. High rooms look out over most aircraft movements if you request an airport-facing room. Can be expensive.

Hyatt Boston Harbor

101 Harborside Drive, Boston, MA 02128
+1 617 568 1234
www.hyatt.com

This tall hotel is very close to runway 14 and the cargo ramp. Its airport-facing rooms look over many of the gates at Terminals A and B, and a good pair of binoculars will catch many of the movements.

Michigan

Detroit Wayne Metropolitan

Days Inn Detroit Metropolitan Airport

9501 Middle Belt Rd, Romulus, MI 48174
+1 734 946 4300
www.daysinn.com

There are lots of hotels and motels to the north of Detroit Metropolitan, and chances are all of them have some kind of view of aircraft approaching from the north. However, the Days Inn is probably the best because it has a view of aircraft arriving on both 22L and R, with the former immediately in front of the other. Ask for a room facing the road. You can't see much on the ground, or using the east-west runways.

Minnesota

Minneapolis St. Paul

SpringHill Suites Minneapolis
St. Paul Airport/Mall of America

2870 Metro Dr, Bloomington, MN 55425
+1 952 854 0300
www.marriott.com

Minneapolis St. Paul is a complex airport with runways and parking areas in all directions. The choice of hotels is also quite limited. However, the SpringHill Suites at the southern end of the airport, near the Mall of America, is acceptable for viewing some movements. The few north-facing rooms look directly into the Delta maintenance hangars, with an awkward view along runway 17/35. Rooms facing west have a good view of aircraft landing on runway 35, but little else.

Missouri

Kansas City

Kansas City Airport Marriott

775 Brasilia Ave, Kansas City, MO 64153
+1 816 464 2200
www.marriott.com

You'll need a top floor room facing west at this hotel to get any views. Although it is set back, you can see across to runway 01L/19R and some of the cargo and maintenance ramps. Sadly many movements from the passenger terminals and the other two runways will be missed.

Nevada

Las Vegas McCarran

La Quinta Inn and Suites Las Vegas South

6560 Surrey Street, Las Vegas, NV 89119
+1 702 492 8900
www.lq.com

This hotel is quite far from the pleasures of The Strip and the big hotels, but it's close to the official spotting area and higher rooms facing the airport will pass close by. Aircraft using the north-south runways are visible in the distance and can be tracked online.

Luxor Hotel and Casino

3900 Las Vegas Blvd South, Las Vegas, NV 89119
+1 702 2624400
www.luxor.com

The pyramid-shaped hotel at the southern end of the Strip has all the amenities you'd hope for, including pools, casino, restaurants and shows. Ask for a room in the pyramid facing the airport. Make sure you're high enough to be above the sphinx outside and you should see all traffic on the 01/19 runways, and the executive jet ramps. An SBS or flight tracking website will help tie up movements on the other runways.

Reno-Tahoe

Hyatt Place Reno-Tahoe Airport

1790 E Plumb Ln, Reno, NV 89502
+1 775 826 2500
www.hyatt.com

Only partial views of aircraft are possible from this hotel, near the car parks. Ask for a high level room facing the airport and you will see some aircraft taxiing to the terminal gates and using the main runways.

New Jersey

Newark Liberty International

Marriott Hotel Newark Airport

1 Hotel Road, Newark, NJ 07114
+1 973 623 0006
www.marriott.com

This hotel is situated in the middle of the terminal complex and has views across the airport from certain rooms, including views of all runways. Rooms reported as excellent are 832, 932, 1032 and 1050. Weekend rates are quite affordable.

Teterboro

Hilton Hasbrouck Heights/Meadowlands

650 Terrace Ave, Hasbrouck Heights, NJ 07604
+1 201 288 6100
www.hilton.com

If you ask for a room on a high floor facing Manhattan, you can get views of aircraft approaching Teterboro. Distant traffic from LaGuardia and Newark can be seen in good weather, too.

New Mexico

Albuquerque International Sunport

Hyatt Place Albuquerque Airport

1400 Sunport Pl SE, Albuquerque, NM 87106
+1 505 242 9300
www.hyatt.com

Arrivals on from the east, on runway 08 can be seen from rooms above ground floor facing the front of this hotel. The aircraft are too distant to photograph, but should be easy enough to identify in daylight conditions. Departures in the opposite 26 direction can be seen, but are generally quite high at this point.

Buffalo Niagara International

Days Hotel Buffalo Airport

4345 Genesee St, Buffalo, NY 14225
+1 716 631 0800
www.daysinn.com

There are a few hotels along Genesee St, behind the passenger terminal and car parks. However, the Days Inn is the best for any kind of views as it is tall and looks out towards the intersection of both runways, and part of the passenger terminal ramp. You'll need to ensure a top floor room facing the busy road for views.

New York JFK

Hilton Garden Inn Queens/JFK

148-18 134th St, Jamaica, NY 11430
+1 718 322 4448
www.hilton.com

This hotel is situated at the western side of the airport, and offers one of the few views of aircraft on the cargo aprons at JFK. You need to request an airport facing room on the highest floor to have a decent view. Runway 13L/31R is the nearest to the hotel, but movements on the others can be seen and logged, especially with the aid of SBS or flight tracking websites. The views can be a little distant for photography. The hotel has a shuttle but linking it to the terminals at JFK, and can also be used to get to LaGuardia Airport.

New York LaGuardia

Courtyard New York LaGuardia

9010 Ditmars Blvd, East Elmhurst, NY 11369
+1 718 446 4800
www.courtyardlaguardia.com

Located close to the terminals and runway 04, this hotel has high rooms looking over the airport from where most movements can easily be logged. Aim for any room between 617 and 628. Photography is possible with a good lens, but not ideal.

Greater Rochester International

Best Western Inn Rochester Airport

395 Buell Rd, Rochester, NY 14624
+1 585 436 4400
www.bestwestern.com

You don't have any views of aircraft on the ground from this hotel, but aircraft landing on the main runway from the north pass directly overhead only seconds before landing. Departures over the hotel can also be seen.

Fairfield Inn Rochester Airport

1200 Brooks Ave, Rochester, NY 14624
+1 585 529 5000
www.marriott.com

This hotel looks out onto one side of the eastern passenger concourse. You'll need to be on the top floor facing the airport, and beware that the road access ramp rises in front of the hotel, so views are not perfect.

Syracuse Hancock International

Best Western Syracuse Airport

900 Col Eileen Collins Blvd, North Syracuse, NY 13212
+1 315 455 7362
www.bestwestern.com

A low, five-sided hotel just to the west of the terminal and north of the cargo apron. Rooms facing south or south-east have fleeting views between the trees and cars of the main runway and taxiway. Useful for keeping an eye on aircraft movements.

Ohio

Cleveland Hopkins

Sheraton Cleveland Airport Hotel

5300 Riverside Dr, Cleveland, OH 44135
+1 216 267 1500
www.sheratonclevelandairport.com

This hotel is centrally located among the terminal complex, alongside the car parks. If you can get a room facing the terminal on one of the top floors you have a view of one of the terminal concourses and gates. Aircraft approaching from the north east are also briefly visible.

Port Columbus

Courtyard Columbus Airport

2901 Airport Dr, Columbus, OH 43219
+1 614 475 8530
www.marriott.com

This hotel is positioned under the approach path between the two parallel runways, a little to the west of the airport. Rooms on the north or south of the hotel face the north or south runways respectively, and balconies make it easy to photograph and log aircraft. To see aircraft on the opposite runway you need to go outside.

Hilton Garden Inn

4265 Sawyer Rd, Columbus, OH 43219
+1 614 231 2869
www.hilton.com

The north wing of this hotel faces the fence line alongside runway 10L/28R. Any aircraft using this runway and its taxiway is easy to see and identify.

Oklahoma

Oklahoma City Will Rogers World Airport

Quality Inn

6300 Terminal Dr, Oklahoma City, OK 73159
+1 405 681 3500
www.qualityinn.com

Rooms along the eastern side of this hotel look towards runway 17L/33R, one of the two main runways for airliner traffic.

Tulsa

Hilton Garden Inn Tulsa Airport

7728 E Virgin Ct, Tulsa, OK 74115
+1 918 838 1444
www.hilton.com

Rooms on the opposite side of the hotel to the car park face towards the final approach to runway 36R. There are no views of the passenger terminal or any of the other runways, however.

Oregon

Portland

Hampton Inn Portland-Airport

8633 NE Airport Way, Portland, OR 97220
+1 503 288 2423
www.hilton.com

One of two hotels at Portland which offer good views of the northern runway, 10L/28R. The Hampton Inn doesn't offer as many rooms with this view, but is generally the more affordable hotel.

Sheraton Portland Airport Hotel

8235 NE Airport Way, Portland, OR 97220
+1 503 281 2500
www.sheraton.com

Like the neighbouring Hampton Inn, the Sheraton has great views (particularly from top floor rooms) overlooking runway 10L/28R. Photography is possible. Ask for a room facing the runway.

Pennsylvania

Philadelphia

Marriott Philadelphia Airport

One Arrivals Road, Philadelphia, PA 19153
+1 215 492 9000
www.marriott.com

Asking for a high room facing the airport should give you a great position looking over aircraft movements at the terminals, and on the runways in the distance. The hotel is linked to Terminal B by a walkway.

Pittsburgh

Hyatt Regency Pittsburgh International Airport

1111 Airport Blvd, Pittsburgh, PA 15231
+1 724 899 1234
www.hyatt.com

This large hotel sits in the middle of the vast car parks outside the main terminal building. It is a tall hotel, so ask for a room on a higher floor. You will only be able to get a view of the northern or southern parallel runways, and not both; the views are probably better of the northern one. There are no views of the terminal area.

Rhode Island

Providence

Comfort Inn

1940 Post Rd, Warwick, RI 02886
+1 401 732 0470
www.choicehotels.com

Ask for an upstairs room facing the airport. Ground floor rooms will be obscured by trees and cars. You will have a view of part of the northern terminal concourse gates and the main runway beyond.

Tennessee

Knoxville McGhee Tyson

Hilton Knoxville Airport

2001 Alcoa Hwy, Alcoa, TN 37701
+1 865 970 4300
www.hilton.com

The closest hotel to the passenger terminal. You'll need a room on the top floor facing the airport to be able to see above the fence and embankment. Your view will be of one of the concourses and the runways in the distance.

Nashville

Embassy Suites by Hilton Nashville Airport

10 Century Blvd, Nashville, TN 37214
+1 615 871 0033
www.hilton.com

This hotel, like most at Nashville, is north of I-40. Therefore you need a room on the top two floors facing the airport to stand a chance of any views. It looks towards runway 13/31, which is not the busiest. You can see distant movements on runway 02L/20R. Rooms 901 – 904 or 934 – 937 are reportedly the best.

Texas

Austin-Bergstrom

Hilton Austin Airport

9515 Hotel Dr, Austin, TX 78719
+1 512 385 6767
www.hilton.com

The main building here is circular, so it's difficult to pick the best room. Those facing east look out onto the final approach to runway 17L. Departures from the reciprocal runway 35R can also be seen.

Dallas Ft. Worth

Grand Hyatt DFW

2337 South International Pkwy, DFW Airport, TX 75261-9045
+1 972 973 1234
granddfw.hyatt.com

This is the best hotel for spotting at DFW, and is located right within the airport complex above Terminal D. If requested, you should be able to obtain a higher room facing the runways. Unfortunately, you'll only be able to see either the east side or west side of the airport, and not both. There is also a rooftop pool with views.

Embassy Suites

4650 W Airport Fwy, Irving, TX 75062
+1 972 790 0093
embassysuites3.hilton.com

This hotel has a number of rooms facing the airport, but is much more distant than the Grand Hyatt. You'll mainly see aircraft arriving and departing, however on the top floor you can see some ground movements too. Some movements also arrive over the hotel.

El Paso

Radisson El Paso

1770 Airway Blvd, El Paso, TX 79925
+1 915 772 3333
www.radisson.com

Rooms along the eastern side of this hotel look out over the general aviation ramps and the retired Southwest Boeing 737-200. You can't see runway or terminal movements, however.

Houston George Bush Intercontinental

Marriott Houston IAH

18700 John F. Kennedy Blvd, Houston, TX 77032
+1 281 443 2310
www.marriott.com

This centrally-located hotel can be expensive, but has some great views. Ask for a high-floor room facing the airport and you shouldn't be disappointed. However, you will only be able to see one side of the action. The windows at the eastern end of the corridors look out towards the cargo apron.

Houston Willam P Hobby

Hampton Inn

> *8620 Airport Blvd, Houston, TX 77061*
> *+1 713 641 6400*
> *www.hamptoninn.com*

An affordable hotel on the edge of the airport perimeter. If you request a north-facing room, you will have a view of any aircraft landing on runway 22. No other parts of the airport are visible.

San Antonio

Super 8

> *11355 San Pedro Avenue, San Antonio, TX 78216*
> *+1 210 342 8488*
> *www.super8.com*

If aircraft are arriving on runways 12L/R, an upper floor room facing the car park at this motel should be sufficient to see aircraft at close quarters just before landing. Affordable and easy to get to.

Utah

Salt Lake City

Microtel Inn & Suites by Wyndham

> *N, 61 Tommy Thompson Rd, Salt Lake City, UT 84116*
> *+1 801 236 2800*
> *www.microtelinn.com*

A small hotel at the south west corner of the airport. Rooms facing east (towards the city) look across the final approach path to both parallel runways used by the majority of airliner traffic. The nearer runway 34L is close enough to photograph aircraft.

Virginia

Richmond

Microtel Inn & Suites by Wyndham

6000 Audubon Dr, Sandston, VA 23150
+1 804 737 3322
www.microtelinn.com

Located on Audubon Drive to the north of the airport. Although there are some obstructions in the way, upper floor rooms facing south have distant views of the airport. What's more, any aircraft arriving on runways 16 or 20 will pass directly overhead at low level.

Washington Dulles

Marriott Dulles Airport

45020 Aviation Drive, Dulles, VA 20166
+1 703 661 8714
www.marriott.com

Situated in the central airport area, this hotel is probably your best bet for any aircraft views. If you request a room facing the adjacent lake, you will see arrivals on runway 19L from a distance.

Washington Reagan National

Residence Inn Arlington Capital View

2850 S Potomac Ave, Arlington, VA 22202
+1 703 415 1300
www.marriott.com

Upper floor corner rooms at this hotel (one of many in Crystal City, but probably the best for aircraft views) have limited views across to the southern end of the airport and its passenger terminals. Aircraft arriving from or departing to the south can be seen, but you'll need flight tracking to help you tie them up.

Washington

Seattle Tacoma

Coast Gateway Hotel

18415 Pacific Highway South, Seattle, WA 98158
+1 206 248 8200
www.coasthotels.com

Situated just across the road from gate A14. Rooms on floor 5 and higher have views of the approach from the south and parts of the ramp (when large aircraft don't obscure the view). Reasonable prices.

DoubleTree Hotel Seattle Airport

18740 International Blvd, Seattle, WA 98188
+1 206 246 8600
www.hilton.com

This hotel has 12 floors and rooms facing the airport on the higher floors have partial views of the parking apron and runways beyond. You can usually see most movements, and closer aircraft can easily be read off. Still a little distant for photography.

Seattle/Everett Paine Field

Hilton Garden Inn Seattle North/Everett

8401 Paine Field Blvd, Mukilteo, Washington, 98275
+1 425 423 9000
www.hilton.com

The Hilton Garden Inn Seattle North/Everett is situated alongside the Future of Flight. Any east-facing room should have views of the runway and part of the flight line.

Roanoke

MainStay Suites

5080 Valley View Blvd NW, Roanoke, VA 24012
+1 540 527 3030
www.choicehotels.com

Rooms facing east at this hotel look out on the final approach to runway 34. Aircraft are quite low here as they pass the hotel, so perfect for viewing. There are no views of the airport or the other runway.

Vietnam

Ho Chi Minh City

Star City Saigon Hotel

144 Nguyễn Văn Trỗi, 8, Phú Nhuận, Ho Chi Minh City 10000
+84 8 3999 8888

This smart hotel is just over a mile from the airport. Rooms on the top floors have a partial view of the runway, and most departing traffic can be seen. It is too far away to photograph, but can be tied up using flight tracking software.

Also from Matt Falcus

Other spotting guide book available from the same author now:

World Airports Spotting Guides

ISBN 978-0-9930950-3-0

Detailed spotting guides to over 300 worldwide airports in the latest update of our popular Airport Spotting Guides series.

World Airport Spotting Guides has collated spotting tips and information for the aviation enthusiast to airports in countries around the world. Learn where to watch aircraft, take photographs, which hotels are good for spotting, and what you're likely to see. Also learn where not to go and where the hobby is not understood.

Airport Spotting Guides Europe

ISBN 978-0-9567187-2-3

Airport Spotting Guides Europe is the most concise and detailed book available on spotting at European airports. Includes spotting details at over 40 of Europe's most notable and worthwhile airports to visit.

Each of the featured airports has a map and detailed descriptions of spotting and photographic locations, plus information on airlines, frequencies, runways, statistics, and important contact details. Another interesting inclusion is a list of recommended hotels at each airport, and details of the aircraft views at each.

Airport Spotting Guides Far East & Australasia

ISBN 978-0-9567187-1-6

Written with the travelling aviation enthusiast and photographer in mind, the book covers essential details at some of the most notable and worthwhile airports to visit in the Far East.

Each of the featured airports has a map and detailed descriptions of spotting and photographic locations, plus information on airlines, frequencies, runways, statistics, and important contact details. Another interesting inclusion is a list of recommended hotels at each airport, and details of the aircraft views at each.

Airport Spotting Hotels

Airport Spotting Guides USA

ISBN 978-0-9559281-8-5

This book covers essential spotting details at America's most notable airports, including locations, hotels, attractions, airlines and statistics.

Each of the 70 featured airports has a map and detailed descriptions of spotting and photographic locations, plus information on airlines, frequencies, runways, statistics, and important contact details. Another interesting inclusion is a list of recommended hotels at each airport, and details of the aircraft views at each.

Lightning Source UK Ltd.
Milton Keynes UK
UKOW06f1824190816

281097UK00027B/776/P